10th Editi
National 1
Coach Han

British Bus Publishing

Body codes used in the Bus Handbook series:

Type:

A	Articulated vehicle
B	Bus, either single-deck or double-deck
BC	Interurban - high-back seated bus
C	Coach
M	Minibus with design capacity of 16 seats or less
N	Low-floor bus (Niederflur), either single-deck or double-deck
O	Open-top bus (CO = convertible - PO = partial open-top)

Seating capacity is then shown. For double-decks the upper deck quantity is followed by the lower deck.

Please note that seating capacities shown are generally those provided by the operator. It is common practice, however, for some vehicles to operate at different capacities when on certain duties.

Door position:-

C	Centre entrance/exit
D	Dual doorway.
F	Front entrance/exit
R	Rear entrance/exit (no distinction between doored and open)
T	Three or more access points

Equipment:-

T	Toilet	TV	Training vehicle.
M	Mail compartment	RV	Used as tow bus or engineers' vehicle.

Allocation:-

s	Ancillary vehicle
t	Training bus
u	out of service or strategic reserve; refurbishment or seasonal requirement
w	Vehicle is withdrawn and awaiting disposal.

e.g. - B32/28F is a double-deck bus with thirty-two seats upstairs, twenty-eight down and a front entrance/exit., N43D is a low-floor bus with two or more doorways.

Re-registrations:-

Where a vehicle has gained new index marks the details are listed at the end of each fleet showing the current mark, followed in sequence by those previously carried starting with the original mark.

Annual books are produced for the major groups:

The Stagecoach Bus Handbook
The First Bus Handbook
The Arriva Bus Handbook
The Go-Ahead Bus Handbook
The National Express Coach Handbook
Some editions for earlier years are available. Please contact the publisher.

Regional books in the series:

The Scottish Bus Handbook
The Welsh Bus Handbook
The Ireland & Islands Bus Handbook
English Bus Handbook: Smaller Groups
English Bus Handbook: Notable Independents
English Bus Handbook: Coaches

Associated series:

The Hong Kong Bus Handbook
The Malta Bus Handbook
The Leyland Lynx Handbook
The Postbus Handbook
The Mailvan Handbook
The Toy & Model Bus Handbook - Volume 1 - Early Diecasts
The Fire Brigade Handbook (fleet list of each local authority fire brigade)
The Police Range Rover Handbook

Some earlier editions of these books are still available. Please contact the publisher on 01952 255669.

Contents

At the time of writing Epsom Coaches are using four coaches in their own livery. Representing them is FJ11GLF, seen in this view pausing at Dudley bus station. *Mark Lyons*

The National Express Coach Handbook

The National Express Coach Handbook is part of the Bus Handbook series that details the fleets of selected bus and coach operators. These Bus Handbooks are published by British Bus Publishing. Although this book has been produced with the encouragement of, and in co-operation with National Express management, it is not an official publication. The vehicles included are subject to variation, particularly as new vehicle deliveries lead to older vehicles being withdrawn. The contents are correct to November 2015.

The Bus Handbook series is concerned primarily with operators fleets and this volume features the coaches operated by contractors on National Express services. The National Express bus operations are included in the 'English Bus Handbook - Groups' book.

Quality photographs for inclusion in the series are welcome, for which a fee is paid. High-resolution digital images of six megapixels or higher are also welcome on CD, DVD or memory stick.

To keep the fleet information up to date we recommend the magazine, Buses, published monthly by Key Publications, or for more detailed information, the PSV Circle monthly news sheets. The writer and publisher would be glad to hear from readers should any information be available which corrects or enhances that given in this publication.

Principal Editor: Stuart Martin.

Acknowledgments: We are grateful to Brian Bannister, Stephen Byrne, Matthew Goggins, Colin Lloyd, Mark Lyons, Malcolm Tranter, the PSV Circle and the management and officials of National Express for their kind assistance and co-operation in the compilation of this book.

The front cover photograph is by Mark Lyons, frontispiece is by Mark Doggett while the rear cover views are by Dave Heath.

Earlier editions are available though our website

ISBN 9781904875 80 2   © Published by British Bus Publishing Ltd, November 2015

British Bus Publishing Ltd, 16 St Margaret's Drive, Telford, TF1 3PH

Telephone: 01952 255669

web; www.britishbuspublishing.co.uk
e-mail: sales@britishbuspublishing.co.uk

NATIONAL EXPRESS

National Express Ltd, National Express House,
Birmingham Coach Station, Mill Lane, Birmingham B5 6DD

A full history of National Express

Although stagecoaches were undoubtedly the forerunners of the present long-distance coach network, it was not until after the First World War and the introduction of motor buses that express coach services really came into their own.

In 1919, Elliott Bros., whose coaches carried the famous 'Royal Blue' fleet name, and who had actually run one of the earlier horse-drawn services, introduced a limited form of express coach service operating between Bournemouth and London. However, Greyhound Motors of Bristol is generally acknowledged as being the first to introduce a daily, all year round, motorised express coach service in Britain. This service which was introduced in 1925 linked Bristol with London and expanded rapidly. Many other operators, able to see the commercial benefits of long-distance travel, introduced similar services in the following months.

The 1930 Road Traffic Act introduced a system of licensing that covered drivers, conductors and the routes that were operated. The implementaion of the Act successfully brought order to a chaotic, rapidly growing, and somewhat haphazard industry. Intending bus and coach operators now found it much harder to introduce new services, with each application for a new or revised service requiring a lengthy process to the local government appointed Traffic Commissioner. This new system of licensing provided the stability for expansion and early co-operation amongst coach operators gave rise to the formation of the first networks of co-ordinated services.

These 'Pool' networks greatly increased travel opportunities for the rapidly growing number of coach passengers. On 1 July 1934, Elliott Brothers became a founder member of the Associated Motorways pool based at Cheltenham. The company's services to the Midlands became AM services and were operated by Royal Blue coaches. Another 'pool' was London Coastal Coaches, based at Victoria Coach Station, which had opened two years earlier in 1932, replacing the original 'London' terminus in Lupus Street of 1924 vintage.

Although most express coaches were suspended in 1942 for the remainder of WW2, some Royal Blue services continued to run to help serve southern areas that were not well served by local bus services. After the war, the full network gradually resumed from April 1946 with new coach designs helping to increase passenger numbers.

A New Era Dawns

The steady increase in the number of coach passengers peaked in the late 1950s followed by a gradual decline due to the rising popularity of private cars. In 1959 the opening of the first stretches of Britain's new motorway network brought new opportunities for coach operators such as Midland Red of Birmingham and Ribble of Preston including the Gay Hostess double-deck coaches.

By the late 1960s most bus companies, with the exception of municipal and small independent operators had formed into two main groups, the state-owned Tilling Group and the British Electric Traction Group (BET). In March 1968, the government brought both groups together under the Transport Holding Company.

The 1968 Transport Act brought about an integrated public passenger transport system across the country. One of the major provisions of the Act was the formation, on 28 November 1968, of the National Bus Company (NBC). NBC began operating on 1 January 1969 and, by 31 December 1969, NBC controlled ninety-three bus companies grouped into forty-four operating units employing 81,000 staff and having a fleet of 21,000 vehicles. A new era of public transport had arrived.

Network Developments

From the beginning, the Directors of what was the biggest road passenger transport operation in Europe began to bring together the coaching activities of each constituent operator. The reasons were obvious. Each local company was pursuing its own policy of express coach service operation.

Inevitably this was leading to duplication of services and it was soon decided that a co-ordinated policy of express coach service planning would be of benefit to the customer and the National Bus Company alike. However regulation of services prevented any real expansion of services or the provision of routes where there were mass markets.

The 'National' brand name was introduced during 1972 and the original 'all white' livery began to appear on coaches as a first stage in offering customers a nationwide standard and a recognisable product. The winter of 1973-74 saw the publication of the first comprehensive coach timetable that included details of the entire 'National' network.

The brand name, National Express, first appeared on publicity in 1974 and on vehicles in 1978. Oddly, some services, such as Oxford to London, were not included in the National network.

In 1979, NBC commissioned a major programme of market research called 'Coachmap'. Every passenger on every journey was asked where, when and why he or she was travelling. The substantial amount of information obtained gave a much needed insight into the travel requirements of both young and old, but was never actually implemented, as the 1980 Transport Act altered the whole of the network.

Deregulation and Expansion

The introduction of the 1980 Transport Act on 6th October swept away fifty years of licensing restrictions and introduced competition on long-distance coach routes.

National Express, and the main Scottish express coach operator, Scottish Citylink, faced new competition from a host of established bus and coach operators trying their hand at operating regular long-distance coach services. It came as no surprise to National Express to discover that many of the 'new' operators seemed to want to run coaches only at the busiest times and only on the most popular routes. The future of the nationwide coach network, and of National Express itself, was in jeopardy.

Totally without subsidy, and by introducing new services and lower fares, National Express fought to win or perish in the ensuing battle. Most of the new operators were unable to sustain continued viable operation and withdrew from operating their services within a matter of months. Even the co-operative venture mounted countrywide under the title 'British Coachways' failed to capture sufficient business.

The strengths of the nationwide, co-ordinated network operated by National Express became all too apparent and the publicity surrounding the coach war gave a major boost to the long-term fortunes of National Express. Passengers also benefited from the new services and lower fares and the skirmish gave National Express valuable experience that was to prove useful in the years to come. Most importantly National Express was free to provide coach services wherever it felt that there was a market.

Annual passenger figures for the nationwide express coach network increased from 8.5 million in 1979 to around fifteen million in 1986 as a direct result of post-deregulation competition.

The annual figure is now around twenty one million and has continued to grow over the last few years. The main variance is that the summer peaks that were experienced on some of the more popular services have now disappeared while all the UK coach services are much busier throughout the whole of the year.

'Rapide' growth

With skilful marketing and an eye for the needs of the customer, a handful of independent coach operators fared better than most. Both Trathens from the West Country and Cotters from Scotland (later to become Stagecoach) introduced up-market services operated by coaches carrying hostesses, refreshments and toilets.

Seeing the opportunities that such an operation would present on other services, National Express entered into an agreement with Trathens to co-operate in running the West Country services. This new concept of improved customer care and service quality was given the name 'Rapide'. The Rapide service introduced a hostess/steward service of light refreshments to each seat. The coaches used on the service were fitted with their own toilet/washroom, air suspension and reclining seats. The on-board facilities cut out the need for time consuming refreshment and toilet stops, offering an instant saving in journey times of around 20%.

The introduction of Rapide services also brought about the first 'seat reservation' system for National Express. Rapide was launched in 1984 and allowed passengers to reserve seats on specific services. Seat reservations were a revolution in public transport at that time as free-sale bookings often led to overloads. This booking system was further developed in 1987 as a full reservation system across the whole National Express network and renamed 'EXTRA'. It was completely redeveloped in 1998 as part of a Year 2000 project.

Public demand for the new Rapide services was high and brought about the introduction of a new design of double-deck coach to cater for the higher number of customers discovering the many benefits of coach travel for the first time. The demand for on-board catering was seen to be declining in the late 1990s with customer surveys showing that passengers were choosing to bring their own style of refreshments with them for their journey. This, coupled with improvements to catering outlets at key coach and bus stations, resulted in a gradual withdrawal of this facility over a number of years. The on-board catering facility on the few remaining National Express services to offer this service were withdrawn at the start of the 2001 Summer timetable.

The continuing provision of on-board washroom/toilet facilities on all National Express coach services meant that in many cases the running time of these service was unaffected by these changes.

'National Express' is Born

On 26 October 1986, following the introduction of the 1985 Transport Act there was deregulation within the industry to all local bus services. Although designed to increase competition between all bus and coach operators there was surprisingly little change in the long-distance express coach market, itself deregulated back in 1980.

However, of greater importance to National Express was the requirement that the National Bus Company should be sold into the private sector. The first subsidiary, National Holidays, was sold in July 1986; the last, London Country (North East) in April 1988.

National Express itself was the subject of a management buy-out, led by Clive Myers, on 17 March 1988. Between 1988 and 1991, National Express Holdings Ltd, the name of the company set up to buy National Express from the National Bus Company, acquired the established North Wales bus and coach operator, Crosville Wales, the Merseyside based coach operator, Amberline, the ATL Holdings Group (which included the Carlton PSV vehicle dealership and the Yelloway Trathen bus and coach company mentioned earlier) and the express coach services of Stagecoach Holdings Ltd based in Perth.

It was during this period that National Express, Plaxton and Volvo created a new purpose-built coach, the Expressliner, which was unveiled on 20 March 1989. The Expressliner, with a kneeling suspension and many other features unique to National Express, brought a new standard of high quality to coach travel across all routes as well as offering the customers a standard product.

This was followed by a second generation Expressliner in 2002 which offered more choice in some of the mechanical features for operators, but still provided the standardisation and comfort for customers.

A Highland 'Fling'

The acquisition of the express coach services of the Stagecoach Holdings Group on 31 July 1989, came at the same time as the long-standing agreement with Scottish Citylink coaches on joint operation across the English/Scottish border came to an end. A new National Express network within Scotland was then introduced under a new brand called Caledonian Express. With Head Offices based at the old Stagecoach premises at Walnut Grove in Perth, the Caledonian Express services linked into the main National Express network and the number of new passengers began to grow immediately. New double-deck coaches entered service on the prestigious Rapide services linking London with Scotland and new marketing initiatives were developed offering a high quality of coach service to and from Scotland for the first time.

In 1993 National Express Group also acquired Scottish Citylink and absorbed the Caledonian Express services into it. This acquisition enabled the Group to offer a truly 'national' coach network with services operating throughout England, Scotland and Wales. However, in August 1998, following the award in April of the franchise to operate ScotRail, Scotland's national railway, National Express Group disposed of Scottish Citylink to Metroline in a deal which left the operation intact and which guaranteed the continuation of cross-border coach travel for a period of time.

The National Express Group 'ScotRail' franchise expired in October 2004 and now National Express operates frequent long distance coaches between the main Scottish cities to all parts of the UK; with connections at London onto the wider European destinations offered by the Eurolines network.

Coaches Can 'Float'

Throughout its long and varied history, National Express has faced many changes. On 23 July 1991, a consortium made up of a number of City investment companies and the Drawlane Transport Group bought out National Express Holdings Ltd.

The chairman of the Drawlane Transport Group, Ray McEnhill, moved from that position and became the Chief Executive of the new company, the National Express Group Limited. Crosville Wales and Amberline were not included in the deal. On 1 December 1992, National Express took another change of direction when Chief Executive Ray McEnhill and deputy chief executive Adam Mills led National Express Group on to the Stock Market through the London Stock Exchange at a share price of 165p.

The prospectus issued at the time of the flotation made the Group's new strategy for development clear. Its objectives were to re-focus and improve the profitability of the core coach business, develop new products and services within its existing operations and acquire new businesses in the passenger transport market. It was during this period that development of a centralised call-centre structure, with one national number, commenced and the first steps were taken on establishing what is now the very successful website.

Group Growth

The National Express Group's policy is to expand the group further by acquisitions within associated areas of the travel industry. This expansion continues to take place not only in the UK but also within Europe and overseas. The National Express Group currently has interests in the UK, North America, Germany, and Spain and Morocco.

United Kingdom

The Group has expansive operations in coach, bus and train operating companies within the UK. These include coach brands such as National Express, Airlinks and Eurolines and bus operations that include West Midlands, Coventry, Dundee, and The Midland Metro. National Express Group also operates the following train franchises in the UK: c2c, the UK's most reliable rail service. Stansted Express and National Express East Anglia. In November 2007, The Kings Ferry company was acquired. It is known for its high-quality coach hire and commuter services from Kent to London and continues to operate with its own identity. In November 2013 The Kings Ferry launched new commuter services from North Somerset into Bristol.

North America

In North America the company also operates Durham School Services which provides student transportation throughout the USA and Stock Transportation which provides student transportation in two provinces of Canada.

Germany

National Express operates scheduled coach services between a number of major cities in Germany through the city2city business. The business was launched in April 2013 and operates services between major cities including Frankfurt, Cologne, Düsseldorf and Munich. It has also been awarded two contracts to serve cities including Cologne and Bonn in Germany's most populous region, North Rhine-Westphalia. The contracts are for a regional express service between Rheine-Münster-Cologne-Krefeld and a Bonn-Cologne-Wuppertal stopping service.

The services are currently run by Deutsche Bahn and carry around eighteen million passengers per year. National Express will start operating the fifteen year contract in December 2015, after first procuring thirty-six new electric trains on behalf of the local authorities.

Spain

In January 2006 National Express Group also acquired Alsa, a transport company which provides coach and bus services throughout Spain with operations also in Portugal and Morocco. Subsequently Continental Auto was also acquired making National Express by far the largest provider of express coach services in Spain.

Coach Stations

During 1994 the first purpose built coach station to be constructed in Britain for over twenty-five years was opened in Norton Street, Liverpool. This new facility, which was widely acclaimed, greatly increased the number of customers using National Express coach services from that area.

Similar increases in passenger numbers were to be seen when new coach stations were opened by National Express at Leeds in 1996, Southampton in 1998, Manchester Central in 2002, Newcastle-upon-Tyne during Spring 2003 and Heathrow's impressive new Central Bus Station which opened in Spring 2006.

The jewel in the crown, is the new Birmingham Coach Station, which was opened in December 2009 by Fabio Capello, the then England football manager. The company is also operating the new Milton Keynes Coachway which opened in December 2010, although this was not constructed by National Express.

Ticketing

Improvements have also been made to assist customers who want to find out about National Express services and who then want to make credit card bookings by phone, by kiosk and via the internet. The new Customer Contact Centre, opened by the Minister of Transport John Spellar in July 2001, based in central Birmingham, offers passengers the very latest in Call Centre Technology. Centralising this activity on just one site offered major benefits to passengers and enables National Express to offer an improved customer service. It has never been easier for customers to book a National Express ticket. Customers can contact the call centre, visit the website, buy tickets from ticket desks or ticket kiosks at stations or visit any one of the 800 National Express ticket agents around the UK. It is now a truly 24/7 sales operation as from 2011 the Call Centre went to 24 hour operation.

National Express was also one of the first UK travel companies to recognise the importance of the internet for customers wishing to obtain both travel information and to book coach tickets at any time of the day, and from anywhere in the world. Passengers booking on-line also benefit from Funfares which offer travel from just £1 per single journey and are now available on most of the main services. Online sales are the most important sales mode.

The nationalexpress.com website now handles over thirty-eight million page views per month with an impressive 276,000 viewings on a peak day, and has won many awards over the last few years. The introduction of 'e-tickets' induring 2002 has also been warmly welcomed by customers, allowing them both to book and print their own coach ticket from the comfort of their home or work with coach drivers simply checking the unique reference number issued with each booking.

During 2006, m-Tickets were also introduced. This innovative ticketing solution alloweds customers to have the opportunity of booking their tickets by phone or the website and then to receive their ticket as a text message which is shown to the driver on boarding.

Airports take off

Airport coach services have always been an important part of the National Express business and in October 1994 a newly branded service called Airlinks was introduced specifically for the growing airport market. It was first established on the Bradford/Leeds to Heathrow/Gatwick corridor. This was followed in May 1995 with the introduction of Airlinks services on corridors between Newcastle/Nottingham to Heathrow/Gatwick, Swansea/Cardiff to Heathrow/Gatwick and Bristol to Heathrow/Gatwick. Early in 1996 the acquisition of the Flightlink brand saw the inclusion of new airport corridors from the West Midlands to Heathrow, Gatwick and Manchester airports. This was followed by the re-branding of all dedicated airport corridors to Flightlink and the launch of the Flightlink network to the retail travel trade.

In mid-1997 Speedlink Airport Services commenced operation of Hotel Hoppa, serving all thirteen hotels located around Heathrow. This major operation, using thirty low-floor buses was a major partnership between Speedlink, BAA and the Heathrow airport hoteliers, and succeeded in reducing traffic congestion in the Heathrow central area by over 30%.

Following a decision made in mid-1998 to bring together the airport operations of Speedlink Airport Services Ltd and the NEL airport services brand of Flightlink, a new company was formed on 1 January 1999 called AirLinks the Airport Coach Company Limited. Its aim was to focus on airport-scheduled and contract bus and coach services and operated vehicles with distinctive liveries such as Flightlink, Speedlink and Jetlink. The airport coach service network continued to grow with AirLinks acquiring all third-party interests in the Jetlink brand, Silverwing Transport Services, Cambridge Coach Services Ltd, Airbus and Capital Logistics; all of which provided coach and bus operations within the Stansted, Luton, Heathrow and Gatwick airports. AirLinks soon became the largest operator of both scheduled and contract services to BAA and the airline operators. But changes to these airport services and other National Express routes were soon to take place.

The main deliveries of new coaches continue with Caetano Levanté bodywork supplied on a mix of two and three axle models from Volvo and Scania. Volvo B11R BN64FKY is one of the latest to be added to the Edwards fleet and seen arriving in London on service 509 from Cardiff. *Mark Lyons*

Revised Look

After many years of acquiring different coach businesses, National Express had actually become an organisation that was operating under many different brand names. Flightlink, Jetlink, Speedlink, Express Shuttle, GoByCoach, Airbus etc seemed at times to be competing with one another. Something needed to happen to bring all these businesses together.

On 03/03/03 National Express revealed its then new corporate identity which included a new logo and new coach livery. The launch, which coincided with the thirtieth anniversary of National Express, took place at Alexandra Palace in London. It was warmly welcomed by the invited press with comments such as 'The new image builds on traditional values but adds a mood of optimism' and 'It isn't until you see the new livery and logo that it occurs to you that the old familiar one has become rather stale,' being offered in support of the changes.

A further identity change was revealed in spring 2008, when a new corporate scheme for all the UK coach, bus and rail operations was revealed.

Pending the arrival of a pair of new coaches, The Traveller's Choice has been using PO12GWP on National Express service 333 from Blackpool. As we go to press Skills, Jim Hughes, Chalfont Northampton (230 service), Johnsons (561), Parks Plymouth (561), Stotts (561) are all interim operators for the former Yourbus work with some using National Express vehicles and some vehicles in their own livery. *Steve Rice*

The Caetano Levanté, available exclusively to National Express and its contracted operators, uses a new 'magic-floor' passenger lift to bring passengers in wheelchairs from the main door to a dedicated space at the front of the coach. This model now makes up the majority of the fleet although there are a few Plaxton Elites to the same specification. All new coaches now have leather seats and at-seat power sockets. Coaches entering service during recent years all coaches are fully DDA accessible. Full details of the bus fleet are included in the 'English Bus Handbook : Smaller Groups' book.

NATIONAL EXPRESS

National Express Ltd, National Express House, Birmingham Coach Station,
Mill Lane, Birmingham, B5 6DD

A1	LA	London - Luton Airport
A3	GW	London - Gatwick Airport
A6	SR	London - Stansted Airport
A6	SH	London - Stansted Airport
A8	SH	London (Liverpool Street Station) - Stansted Airport
A9	SH	London (Stratford) - Stansted Airport
409	WM	London - Aberystwyth University
410	WM	London - Birmingham
444	WM	London - Worcester
504	SR	London - Plymouth
545	WM	London - Pwllheli
561	SR	London - Leeds
701	SR	Aldershot - Woking - Heathrow Airport
727	SR	Norwich - Gatwick Airport - Brighton
747	SR	Brighton - Heathrow Airport
787	SR	Cambridge - Heathrow Airport

8-18			Scania K340 EB6			Caetano Levanté			C61FT	2007		
				11	SH	FN07BYV	**17**	SH	FJ07BZC	**18**	SH	MIG9443
8	SH	FJ07DVO		**15**	SH	FJ07BZA						

26-39			Scania K340 EB6			Caetano Levanté			C61FT	2007		
26	SH	FJ57KHT		**33**	SH	FJ57KHA	**37**	SH	MIG9437	**39**	SH	FJ57KHG
32	SH	SHZ5735		**35**	SH	MIG9438						

102	SH	FJ10EZV	Scania K340 EB4			Caetano Levanté			C49FT	2010		

The fleet number displayed on National Express vehicles is prefixed by depot codes with the SH on number 15, FN07BZA, representing the Stuart Hill depot. It is seen operating Stansted Airport service A6.
Mark Doggett

The Caetano Levanté is similar to a Portuguese market model, Caetano Winner, and was designed exclusively for National Express using a brief given by National Express for 'an easy access vehicle to schedule 1 of the Disability Discrimination Act with the wow factor'. It is currently being supplied on Volvo B8R and Scania K440 in twin-axle form and Volvo B11R and Scania K480 in tri-axle form. Volvo B9R 139, FJ12FYP, is shown. *Mark Lyons*

115-135 Volvo B9R   Caetano Levanté   C48FT   2010-11

115	SR	FJ60HXY	121	SR	FJ11RDV	126	SR	FJ11MKM	131	SR	FJ11MJO
117	SR	FJ11MKL	122	SR	FJ11RDU	127	SR	FJ11MKN	132	SR	FJ11MJU
118	SR	FJ11MKE	123	SR	FJ11MKD	128	SR	FJ11MKU	133	SR	FJ11MJV
119	SR	FJ11MKK	124	SR	FJ11MKF	129	SR	FJ11MKV	134	SR	FJ11MJX
120	SR	FJ11RDO	125	SR	FJ11MKG	130	SR	FJ11MJK	135	SR	FJ11MJY

136-143 Volvo B9R   Caetano Levanté   C48FT   2012

136	SR	FJ12FYL	138	LA	FJ12FYN	140	SR	FJ12FYR	142	SR	FJ12FYO
137	SR	FJ12FYM	139	LA	FJ12FYP	141	SR	FJ12FYH	143	SR	FJ12FXD

145-161 Volvo B9R   Caetano Levanté   C48FT   2013

145	LA	FJ13EBK	149	LA	FJ13EBO	152	LA	FJ13EBV	160	LA	FJ13ECN
						155	LA	FJ13ECA			
146	LA	FJ13EBL	150	LA	FJ13EBP	156	LA	FJ13ECC	161	LA	FJ13ECT
147	LA	FJ13EBM	151	LA	FJ13EBU	159	LA	FJ13ECF			

162-175 Volvo B9R   Caetano Levanté   C48FT   2011   Rotala, 2013

162	GW	FJ11GJO	166	GW	FJ11GKV	170	SR	FJ11MLE	173	SR	FJ11MLL
163	GW	FJ11GJU	167	GW	FJ11GKX	171	LA	FJ11MLF	174	SR	FJ11MLN
164	SR	FJ11GKP	168	SR	FJ11GLK	172	GW	FJ11MLK	175	SR	FJ11MLO
165	GW	FJ11GKU	169	GW	FJ11GLZ						

2014 arrivals include twenty-six Scania K480 tri-axles for its own fleet, all allocated to Stuart Hill. Representing them is 191, BK14LGG, seen near Victoria Coach Station. *Steve Rice*

176-201

		Scania K480 EB6			Caetano Levanté		C57FT	2014		
176	SH	BK14LFP	183	SH	BK14LFX	190	SH	BK14LGF	196	SH	BK14LGU
177	SH	BK14LFR	184	SH	BK14LFY	191	SH	BK14LGG	197	SH	BK14LGV
178	SH	BK14LFS	185	SH	BK14LFZ	192	SH	BK14LGJ	198	SH	BK14LGW
179	SH	BK14LFT	186	SH	BK14LGA	193	SH	BK14LGL	199	SH	BK64FKL
180	SH	BK14LFU	187	SH	BK14LGC	194	SH	BK14LGN	200	SH	BK64FKM
181	SH	BK14LFV	188	SH	BK14LGD	195	SH	BK14LGO	201	SH	BK64FKO
182	SH	BK14LFW	189	SH	BK14LGE						

88321-8352

		ADL Dart 4 9.5m			ADL Enviro 200		N22F	2008		
8321	HO	SN08AAU	8329	HO	SN08ABU	8337	HO	SN08ACV	8345	HO	SN08ADZ
8322	HO	SN08AAV	8330	HO	SN08ABV	8338	HO	SN08ACX	8346	HO	SN08AEA
8323	HO	SN08AAX	8331	HO	SN08ABX	8339	HO	SN08ACY	8347	HO	SN08AEB
8324	HO	SN08AAY	8332	HO	SN08ABZ	8340	HO	SN08ACZ	8348	HO	SN08AEC
8325	HO	SN08AAZ	8333	HO	SN08ACF	8341	HO	SN08ADO	8349	HO	SN08AED
8326	HO	SN08ABF	8334	HO	SN08ACJ	8342	HO	SN08ADU	8350	HO	SN08AEE
8327	HO	SN08ABK	8335	HO	SN08ACO	8343	HO	SN08ADV	8351	HO	SN08AEF
8328	HO	SN08ABO	8336	HO	SN08ACU	8344	HO	SN08ADX	8352	HO	SN08AEG

8354-8358

		ADL E20D 8.8m			ADL Enviro 200		N29F	2012		
8354	HO	MX61BBE	8356	HO	MX61BBJ	8357	HO	MX61BBK	8358	HO	MX61BBN
8355	HO	MX61BBF									

8360-8371

		ADL E20D 8.8m			ADL Enviro 200		N39F	2015		
8360	SR	SN15LKG	8363	SR	SN15LKJ	8366	SR	SN15LKC	8369	SR	SN15LKD
8361	SR	SN15LKE	8364	SR	SN15LKJ	8367	SR	SN15LKM	8370	SR	SN15LKP
8362	SR	SN15LKF	8365	SR	SN15LKK	8368	SR	SN15LKO	8371	SR	SN15LKU

8373-8376

		Optare Solo M900 SR			Optare		N32F	2015		
8373	SR	KX15BLF	8374	SR	KX15BLJ	8375	SR	KX15BLK	8376	SR	KX15BLM

National Express' coaching activities include several contracts based around Heathrow and Gatwick airports. Carrying British Airways livery is Alexander-Dennis Enviro 200 3862, SN15LKF. *Mark Lyons*

8377	SR	SK15HBF	ADL E20D		ADL Enviro 200		N29F	2015	
8378	SR	SK15HBG	ADL E20D		ADL Enviro 200		N29F	2015	
8379	SR	SK15HBH	ADL E20D		ADL Enviro 200		N29F	2015	

8541-8547   Mercedes-Benz Citaro O530 GLE   AN29D   2008

8541	ST	R500LSA	8543	ST	N500LSA	8545	ST	R600LSA	8547 ST T600LSA
8542	ST	T500LSA	8544	ST	P600LSA	8546	ST	S600LSA	

8554-8560   Mercedes-Benz Citaro O530 LE   N22D   2008

8554	ST	K700LSA	8556	ST	P700LSA	8558	ST	T700LSA	8560 ST P800LSA
8555	ST	N700LSA	8557	ST	R700LSA	8559	ST	N800LSA	

8562	SR	KX58GUK	ADL Dart 4		ADL Enviro 200		N25F	2008
8563	SR	KX58GUO	ADL Dart 4		ADL Enviro 200		N25F	2008

8564-8573   Mercedes-Benz Sprinter 515cdi   KVC   M9   2009

8564	WD	KX58BJK	8567	WD	KX58BJO	8570	WD	KX58BFA	8572 WD KX09CJO
8565	WD	KX58BJV	8568	WD	KX58BKA	8571	WD	KX58BJY	8573 WD KX09CJU
8566	WD	KX58BJU	8569	WD	KX58BJZ				

8574-8584   Mercedes-Benz Citaro O530   AN30D   2003-04   Arriva London, 2011

8574	WD	K900LSA	8576	WD	P900LSA	8578	WD	S900LSA	8581 WD T800LSA
8575	WD	N900LSA	8577	WD	R900LSA	8580	WD	S800LSA	8584 WD T900LSA

8600-8605   NAW Cobus 2700s   Cobus   N15T

8600	GW	8600	8602	GW	8602	8604	w	8604	8605 GW 8605
8601	GW	8601	8603	GW	8603				

8606-8622   DAF SB220   East Lancs Myllennium   N29D   2000   Aviation Defence, 2009

8606	GW	X831NWX	8608	GW	X833NWX	8614	GW	X839NWX	8616 GW X841NWX
8607	GW	X832NWX	8612	GW	X837NWX	8615	GW	X840NWX	8617 GW X842NWX

8641-8645   NAW Cobus 2700s   Cobus   N15T   2010

8641	SC	8641	8643	SC	8643	8644	SC	8644	8645 SC 8645
8642	SC	8642							

Luton Airport is now a base as well as a destination for National Express coaches with fourteen Volvo B9Rs based there for route A1. At the London end of the route is 160, FJ13ECN. *Dave Heath*

8646-8657

										Mercedes-Benz Citaro O530			AN30D	2010
8646	GW	BK10EHT	8649	GW	BK10EHW	8652	GW	BK10EHZ	8655	GW	BK10EJX
8647	GW	BK10EHU	8650	GW	BK10EHX	8653	GW	BK10EJU	8656	GW	BK10EJY
8648	GW	BK10EHV	8651	GW	BK10EHY	8654	GW	BK10EJV	8657	GW	BK10EJZ

8658-8663

NAW Cobus 2700s   Cobus   N15T   2010

8658	GW	8658	8660	GW	8660	8662	GW	8662	8663	GW	8663
8659	GW	8659	8661	GW	8661

8667-8677

Ford Transit   Ford   M16   2012

8667	AL	HN62DYV	8670	AL	HN62FMM	8673	AL	HN62FMU	8676	AL	HN62DYX
8668	AL	HN62EAA	8671	AL	HN62FMN	8674	AL	HN62FMV	8677	AL	HN62DYY
8669	AL	HN62FML	8672	AL	HN62FMO	8675	AL	HN62DYW

8678	AL	VO12PBU	Volkswagen Caravelle	Volkswagen	M16	2012	
8679	AL	CN60AKJ	Mercedes-Benz 811D	Mercedes-Benz	M16	2012	
8680	ST	NE03BUS	Mercedes-Benz Citaro O530		AN30D	2008	??, 2015
8681	ST	NE02BUS	Mercedes-Benz Citaro O530		AN30D	2008	
8682	ST	KX08HOA	Mercedes-Benz Vito 511D	Mercedes-Benz	M12	2008	

9084-9089

Volvo B9R   Caetano Levanté   C48FT   2011   On loan from East Yorkshire

9084	WA	FJ11GJX	9086	WA	FJ11GJZ	9088	WA	FJ11GKC	9089	WA	FJ11GLV
9085	WA	FJ11GJY	9087	WA	FJ11GKA

9100-9105

Volvo B9R   Caetano Levanté   C48FT   2015

9100	WA	BK15AJU	9102	WA	BK65WAA	9104	WA	BK65WEJ	9105	-	-
9101	WA	BK15AJV	9103	WA	BK65WAE

Depots and codes: Crawley (Whetstone Close, Tinsley Green) - CY; Bishops Stortford (Start Hill, Great Hollingbury) - SH; Luton Airport - LA and West Drayton (Sipson Road) - WD (buses) and SR (coaches); Stansted Airport - SS. Details of the other National Express fleets may be found in the *English Bus Handbook : Groups Handbook*.

G ABBOT & SONS

G Abbott & Sons. Aumans House, 37 Roman Road, Leeming, Northallerton, DL7 9RZ

561   Bradford - London

No vehicles are contracted in National Express colours. The vehicles used on the services are selected from the main fleet.

AMBASSADOR TRAVEL

Ambassador Travel (Anglia) Ltd, James Watt Close, Gapton Hall Industrial Estate, Great Yarmouth, NR31 0NX

371   Great Yarmouth - Birmingham
490   London - Norwich (University of East Anglia)
491   London - Great Yarmouth
491   London - Lowestoft
497   London - Great Yarmouth

206	FJ09DXA	Scania K340 EB4	Caetano Levanté	C49FT	2009
207	FJ09DXB	Scania K340 EB4	Caetano Levanté	C49FT	2009
208	FJ09DXC	Scania K340 EB4	Caetano Levanté	C49FT	2009
209	FJ09DXE	Scania K340 EB4	Caetano Levanté	C49FT	2009
210	BF63ZSK	Volvo B9R	Caetano Levanté	C48FT	2013
211	BF63ZSL	Volvo B9R	Caetano Levanté	C48FT	2013
212	BF63ZSN	Volvo B9R	Caetano Levanté	C48FT	2013

Details of other vehicles in this fleet may be found in the *English Bus Handbook: Coaches* book.

One of three Volvo B9Rs to join Ambassador's fleet in 2013 is 212, BF63ZSN. *Mark Doggett*

BENNETT'S

Bennetts Coaches, Eastern Avenue, Gloucester, GL4 4LP

444   Gloucester - London

BG1	BF63ZRL	Volvo B9R	Caetano Levanté	C48FT	2013
BG2	BK14LDV	Volvo B9R	Caetano Levanté	C48FT	2014
BG3	BK14LDX	Volvo B9R	Caetano Levanté	C48FT	2014
BG4	BK14LDY	Volvo B9R	Caetano Levanté	C48FT	2014
BG5	BK14LDZ	Volvo B9R	Caetano Levanté	C48FT	2014

BL TRAVEL

B Lockwood, The Garage, Hoyle Mill Road, Kinsley, Wakefield WF9 5JB

561   London - Bradford

No vehicles are contracted in National Express colours. The vehicles used on the services are selected from the main fleet.

2014 saw a fleet update for Bennett's with the arrival of further Volvo coaches. Heathrow airport is the location for this view of BK14LDV on a Gloucester-bound journey on route 444. National Express allocates fleet numbers to most coaches used on the network, some of which are carried on the vehicles. *Dave Heath*

BRUCE'S

J Bruce, 40 Main Street, Salsburgh, ML7 4LA

336	Edinburgh - Plymouth
532	Edinburgh - Plymouth
539	Edinburgh - Bournemouth
588	Inverness - London
590	Aberdeen - Glasgow - London

FN63PWJ	Scania K340 EB6	Caetano Levanté	C61FT	2013
FN63PWK	Scania K340 EB6	Caetano Levanté	C61FT	2013
FN63PWL	Scania K340 EB6	Caetano Levanté	C61FT	2013
FN63PWO	Scania K340 EB6	Caetano Levanté	C61FT	2013
FN63PWU	Scania K340 EB6	Caetano Levanté	C61FT	2013
FN63PWX	Scania K340 EB6	Caetano Levanté	C61FT	2013
FN63PWY	Scania K340 EB6	Caetano Levanté	C61FT	2013
FN63PWZ	Scania K340 EB6	Caetano Levanté	C61FT	2013
FJ14GPV	Scania K340 EB6	Caetano Levanté	C61FT	2013

Details of the other vehicles in this fleet may be found in the *Scottish Bus Handbook*.

Bruce's of Salsburgh provides coaches for some of the longest services on the National Express network with service 588 covering over 920 Kilometres and around 850 Km for Edinburgh to Plymouth. Arriving in Devonshire is the latest fleet addition, FJ14GPV, complete with Scottish Saltier emblem. *Steve Rice*

CHALFONT

Chalfont Coaches of Harrow, 200 Featherstone Rd, Southall UB2 5AQ

023	London - Bexhill				
035	London - Bournemouth				
440	London - Leicester				
450	London - Nottingham				
460	London - Stratford-upon-Avon				
509	London - Cardiff				

CD5	FJ61EWN	Volvo B9R	Caetano Levanté	C48FT	2011
CD6	FJ61EWO	Volvo B9R	Caetano Levanté	C48FT	2011
CD7	BF63ZSG	Volvo B9R	Caetano Levanté	C48FT	2013
CD8	BF63ZSJ	Volvo B9R	Caetano Levanté	C48FT	2013

Details of the vehicles in this fleet may be found in the *English Bus Handbook : Coaches* book

Representing Chalfont Coaches of Harrow is FJ61EWO, seen in Stratford-upon-Avon on service 460 while preparing to leave for London. *Mark Doggett*

CHALFONT

The Coach Station, Short Lane, Cogenhoe, Northampton, NN7 1LE

230		Derby - Gatwick Airport			
455		London - Northampton - Corby			
661		Coventry - Skegness			
707		Northampton - Gatwick Airport			

**	WA57JZT	Volvo B12B	Van Hool T9 Acron	C53FT	2008
CD1	WA59EBC	Volvo B12B	Van Hool T9 Acron	C53FT	2009
*	WA10ENK	Volvo B12B	Van Hool T9 Acron	C53FT	2010
CD2	WA10ENL	Volvo B12B	Van Hool T9 Acron	C53FT	2010
*	WA10ENM	Volvo B12B	Van Hool T9 Acron	C53FT	2010
*	WA60DZG	Volvo B12B	Van Hool T9 Acron	C53FT	2010
*	WA61AKF	Volvo B12B	Van Hool T9 Acron	C53FT	2011
CD3	WA61AKP	Volvo B12B	Van Hool T9 Acron	C53FT	2011
CD4	WA61AKU	Volvo B12B	Van Hool T9 Acron	C53FT	2011
*	WF63LTA	Van Hool TX16 Acron	Van Hool	C53FT	2013
*	WF63LTE	Van Hool TX16 Acron	Van Hool	C53FT	2013
CD8	BK14LEF	Volvo B9R	Caetano Levanté	C48FT	2014
CD9	BK14LEJ	Volvo B9R	Caetano Levanté	C48FT	2014
CD10	BK14LEU	Volvo B9R	Caetano Levanté	C48FT	2014
CD11	BK14LFA	Volvo B9R	Caetano Levanté	C48FT	2014
CD12	BK14LFB	Volvo B9R	Caetano Levanté	C48FT	2014
CD13	BK14LFD	Volvo B9R	Caetano Levanté	C48FT	2014

Details of the vehicles in this fleet may be found in the *English Bus Handbook : Coaches* book

This year Chalfont have taken on more contracts for National Express with several approved vehicles being in all-white (shown ** above) or their own colours (*). Illustrated is Volvo B12B WA59EBC. *Dave Heath*

R W CHENERY

PG Garnham, The Garage, Dickleburgh, Diss, Norfolk, IP21 4NJ

490	London - Norwich (University of East Anglia)
498	London - Long Stratton
813	London - Norwich

FJ06GGK	Volvo B12B	Caetano Levanté	C48FT	2006	On loan from National Express
FJ60HXS	Volvo B9R	Caetano Levanté	C48FT	2010	On loan from National Express
FJ11MKA	Volvo B9R	Caetano Levanté	C48FT	2011	On loan from National Express
FJ11MKC	Volvo B9R	Caetano Levanté	C48FT	2011	On loan from National Express

Details of the vehicles in this fleet may be found in our *English Bus Handbook : Coaches* book

Carrying the destination screen for its arrival in London on service 490 is FJ11MKA. *Mark Doggett*

EAST YORKSHIRE

East Yorkshire Motor Services Ltd, 252 Anlaby Road, Hull, HU3 2RS

031	London - Portsmouth
322	Hull - Swansea
327	Scarborough - Bristol
447	London - Hull
448	London - Peterborough - Hull
449	London - Mablethorpe
484	London - Walton-on-the-Naze
562	London - Hull
563	London - Scarborough

68	YX08FYP	Volvo B12B	Caetano Levanté	C49FT	2008
74	FN62CEA	Volvo B12B	Caetano Levanté	C49FT	2012
75	FN62CEU	Volvo B12B	Caetano Levanté	C49FT	2012
76	FN62CGX	Volvo B12B	Caetano Levanté	C49FT	2012
78	YY63OEJ	Volvo B12B	Caetano Levanté	C49FT	2013
79	YY63OEK	Volvo B12B	Caetano Levanté	C49FT	2013
80	YY63OEL	Volvo B12B	Caetano Levanté	C49FT	2013
81	YY63OEM	Volvo B12B	Caetano Levanté	C49FT	2013
82	YY63OEN	Volvo B12B	Caetano Levanté	C49FT	2013
83	YY63OEO	Volvo B12B	Caetano Levanté	C49FT	2013
84	YY63OJA	Volvo B12B	Caetano Levanté	C49FT	2014
85	YY63OJB	Volvo B12B	Caetano Levanté	C49FT	2014
86	YY63OJC	Volvo B12B	Caetano Levanté	C49FT	2014
87	YY63OJD	Volvo B12B	Caetano Levanté	C49FT	2014

Details of the other vehicles in this fleet may be found in the *English Bus Handbook : Smaller Groups* book.

Representing the East Yorkshire fleet is Volvo B12B 79, YY63OEK. Several of the earlier Caetano Levanté coaches operated by East Yorkshire are now with National Express working from the Walsall bus depot.
Mark Doggett

EDWARDS COACHES

Edwards Coaches Ltd, Newtown Industrial Estate, Llantwit Fardre, Pontypridd, CF38 2EE

201	Swansea - Cardiff - Gatwick Airport
202	Swansea - Cardiff - Heathrow Airport
216	Cardiff - Bristol Airport
320	Cardiff - Bradford
321	Birmingham - Bradford
322	Birmingham - Swansea
343	Birmingham - Swansea
507	Swansea - London
508	London - Haverfordwest
509	London - Swansea - Cardiff
528	Haverfordwest - Rochdale
672	Swansea - Minehead (Butlins)

FJ60HXV   Volvo B9R   Caetano Levanté   C48FT   2010   National Express
FJ60HXX   Volvo B9R   Caetano Levanté   C48FT   2010   National Express

---

Volvo B9R   Caetano Levanté   C48FT   2011

FJ11GKY	FJ11GMX	FJ11GNF	FJ11GNO
FJ11GMO	FJ11GMY	FJ11GNK	FJ11GOH
FJ11GMU	FJ11GMZ	FJ11GNN	

Volvo B9R   Caetano Levanté   C48FT   2012

FJ12FXC	FJ12FXS	FJ12FXY	FJ12FYD
FJ12FXM	FJ12FXU	FJ12FXZ	FJ12FYE
FJ12FXO	FJ12FXV	FJ12FYA	FJ12FYF
FJ12FXP	FJ12FXW	FJ12FYB	FJ12FYG
FJ12FXR	FJ12FXX	FJ12FYC	FJ12FYK

BN64FKY   Volvo B11R   Caetano Levanté   C56FT   2015
BN64FKZ   Volvo B11R   Caetano Levanté   C56FT   2015

Details of the other vehicles in this fleet may be found in the *Welsh Bus Handbook*.

A dragon emblem representing Wales adorns the rear of FJ12FXZ as it catches the evening sun at Hatton Cross on its way to Gatwick airport. *Dave Heath*

EPSOM COACHES - RATP

Epsom Coaches Ltd, Roy Richmond Way, Epsom, KT19 9AF

410	London - Birmingham - Wolverhampton				
540	London - Liverpool				
801	London - Bradford				
802	London - Liverpool				
808	London - Wolverhampton				

EP1	FJ11GLF	Volvo B9R	Caetano Levanté	C48FT	2011
EP2	FJ11GMV	Volvo B9R	Caetano Levanté	C48FT	2011
EP3	FJ61EYK	Volvo B9R	Caetano Levanté	C48FT	2012
EP4	FJ61EYL	Volvo B9R	Caetano Levanté	C48FT	2012

Details of the other vehicles in this fleet may be found in the *English Bus Handbook: Coaches* book

Representing the four coaches used by Epsom Coaches is FJ61EYK, seen in London on the frequent link with Birmingham. *Colin Lloyd*

EXCALIBUR COACHES

Excalibur Coaches Ltd, Nyes Wharf, Frensham Street, London, SE15 6TH

561   London - Bradford

BL14LSO	Volvo B11R	Sunsundegui SC7	C57FT	2014	
BL14LSU	Volvo B11R	Sunsundegui SC7	C57FT	2014	
BL14LSV	Volvo B11R	Sunsundegui SC7	C57FT	2014	
BL14LSX	Volvo B11R	Sunsundegui SC7	C57FT	2014	
YT12YUS	Scania K360 EB6	Irizar i6	C57FT	2012	Princess, West End, 2015
FJ61EXT	Volvo B9R	Caetano Levanté	C48FT	2012	Yourbus, Heanor, 2015
FJ61EXX	Volvo B9R	Caetano Levanté	C48FT	2012	Yourbus, Heanor, 2015

Details of the other vehicles in this fleet may be found in the *English Bus Handbook: Coaches* book

The junction of Buckingham Palace Road and Elizabeth Street is a popular location for pictures of National Express coaches. East Yorkshire's 84, YY63OJA, sets off north for Mablethorpe. *Colin Lloyd*

GALLOWAY

Galloway European Coachlines Ltd, Denter's Hill, Mendlesham, Stowmarket, IP14 5RR

| 250 | Ipswich - Heathrow Airport |
| 481 | London - Felixstowe |

300	FJ61EVN	Volvo B9R	Caetano Levanté	C48FT	2011	
301	FJ61EVP	Volvo B9R	Caetano Levanté	C48FT	2011	
302	FJ61EVR	Volvo B9R	Caetano Levanté	C48FT	2011	
304	FJ61EVU	Volvo B9R	Caetano Levanté	C48FT	2011	
305	FJ61EVV	Volvo B9R	Caetano Levanté	C48FT	2011	
317	FN62CAA	Volvo B9R	Caetano Levanté	C48FT	2012	
341	FJ61EYG	Volvo B9R	Caetano Levanté	C48FT	2012	South Gloucester, 2015
348	BK15AJX	Volvo B8R	Caetano Levanté	C48FT	2015	

Details of the vehicles in this fleet may be found in the *English Bus Handbook : Coaches* book

Pictured while working a northerly journey on route 250 is Galloway's 302, FJ61EVR. *Mark Doggett*

GO NORTH EAST

Go North East Ltd, 117 Queen Street, Bensham, Gateshead, NE8 2UA

024	London - Eastbourne
332	Newcastle-upon-Tyne - Birmingham - Swindon
380	Newcastle-upon-Tyne - Leeds
410	London - Birmingham
420	London - Birmingham
425	London - Newcastle-upon-Tyne
426	London - South Shields
530	Paignton - Newcastle-upon-Tyne
531	Plymouth - Newcastle-upon-Tyne
561	London - Skipton
580	Newcastle-upon-Tyne - Liverpool
591	London - Edinburgh
594	London - Edinburgh
663	Newcastle-upon-Tyne - Skegness (Butlins)

7094-7102   Scania K340 EB6   Caetano Levanté   C53FT   2008

7094	CS	FJ08KLF	7097	CS	FJ08KLX	7099	CS	FJ08KMU	7101	CS	FJ08KNV
7095	CS	FJ08KLS	7098	CS	FJ08KLZ	7100	CS	FJ08KMV	7102	CS	FJ08KNW
7096	CS	FJ08KLU									

| 7103 | CS | JCN822 | Volvo B9R | | | Caetano Levanté | | C48FT | 2012 | | |
| 7104 | CS | 574CPT | Volvo B9R | | | Caetano Levanté | | C48FT | 2012 | | |

7105-7112   Volvo B9R   Caetano Levanté   C48FT   2013

| 7105 | CS | BF63ZPV | 7107 | CS | BF63ZPY | 7109 | CS | BF63ZRA | 7111 | CS | BF63ZRY |
| 7106 | CS | BF63ZPW | 7108 | CS | BF63ZPZ | 7110 | CS | BF63ZRC | 7112 | CS | BF63ZRZ |

7113-7117   Volvo B9R   Caetano Levanté   C48FT   2011   Yourbus, 2013

| 7113 | CS | FJ60GJY | 7115 | CS | FJ60HYB | 7116 | CS | FJ60KVM | 7117 | CS | FJ60KVO |
| 7114 | CS | FJ60HXW | | | | | | | | | |

Previous registrations:

574CPT	FJ61GZD		JCN822	FJ61GZC

Details of the other vehicles in this fleet may be found in the annual *Go-Ahead Bus Handbook*.

Calling in at York on its way to South Shields in service 426 is Go Northern's 7104, 574CPT, one of two to carry 'Cherished' index numbers. *Mark Lyons*

GO SOUTH COAST

Wilts & Dorset Bus Co. Ltd, Towngate House, 2-8 Parkstone Road, Poole, BH15 2PR

033	London - Salisbury - Yeovil
035	London - Bournemouth University
205	Heathrow Airport - Poole
206	Gatwick Airport - Poole
806	London - Poole

914	FJ60EHB	Volvo B9R	Caetano Levanté	C48FT	2010	Excelsior, 2015
915	FJ60EHC	Volvo B9R	Caetano Levanté	C48FT	2010	Excelsior, 2015
916	FJ60EHD	Volvo B9R	Caetano Levanté	C48FT	2010	Excelsior, 2015
917	FJ60EHE	Volvo B9R	Caetano Levanté	C48FT	2010	Excelsior, 2015
918	FJ60EHF	Volvo B9R	Caetano Levanté	C48FT	2010	Excelsior, 2015
919	FJ11GNP	Volvo B9R	Caetano Levanté	C48FT	2011	Excelsior, 2015
920	FJ11GNU	Volvo B9R	Caetano Levanté	C48FT	2011	Excelsior, 2015
921	FJ11GNV	Volvo B9R	Caetano Levanté	C48FT	2011	Excelsior, 2015
922	FJ11GNX	Volvo B9R	Caetano Levanté	C48FT	2011	Excelsior, 2015
923	FJ11GNY	Volvo B9R	Caetano Levanté	C48FT	2011	Excelsior, 2015
924	FJ11GNZ	Volvo B9R	Caetano Levanté	C48FT	2011	Excelsior, 2015
925	FJ61EWX	Volvo B9R	Caetano Levanté	C48FT	2012	Excelsior, 2015
926	FJ61EWY	Volvo B9R	Caetano Levanté	C48FT	2012	Excelsior, 2015
7052	BF63ZSO	Volvo B9R	Caetano Levanté	C48FT	2013	
7053	BF63ZSP	Volvo B9R	Caetano Levanté	C48FT	2013	

Details of the other vehicles in this fleet may be found in the annual *Go-Ahead Bus Handbook*.

HAMILTONS COACHES

Hamiltons Coaches, 3 Fox St, Rothwell, Kettering, NN14 6AN

397	Leicester - Blackpool

No vehicles are contracted in National Express colours. The vehicles used on the services are selected from the main fleet.

Latterly with Excelsior, Go-Ahead now operate on these services, taking in the coaches too. 920, FJ11GNU, is seen at Bournemouth station.
Mark Lyons

JIM HUGHES COACHES

Jim Hughes Ltd, Wear St, Sunderland, Tyne and Wear SR5 2BH

425	London - Ashington
426	London - South Sheilds
435	London - Ashington
436	London - South Shields

FH06EBM	Volvo B12B	Caetano Levanté	C49FT	2006	On loan from National Express
FN06FMA	Volvo B12B	Caetano Levanté	C49FT	2006	On loan from National Express
FJ57KHP	Volvo B12B	Caetano Levanté	C49FT	2007	On loan from National Express
FJ57KHR	Volvo B12B	Caetano Levanté	C49FT	2007	On loan from National Express

JOHNSONS BROS

Johnsons Bros, Green Acres, Green Lane, Hodthorpe, Worksop, S80 4XR

349	Nottingham - Stansted Airport
350	Liverpool - Mansfield - Stansted Airport
561	London - Bradford

FJ60EGE	Volvo B9R	Caetano Levanté	C48FT	2010	
FJ60EGF	Volvo B9R	Caetano Levanté	C48FT	2010	
FJ12FXA	Volvo B9R	Caetano Levanté	C48FT	2012	E Stott, 2013

Details of the vehicles in this fleet may be found in the *English Bus Handbook : Coaches* book

LLEW JONES

Llew Jones International, Station Yard, Station Rd, Llanrwst, LL26 0EH

| 385 | Bangor - Manchester |

| LJ12LLJ | Volvo B9R | Caetano Levanté | C48FT | 2012 |

Other vehicles used on the service are selected from the main fleet.

LUCKETTS

H Luckett & Co Ltd, Broadcut, Wallington, Fareham, PO16 8TB

025	London - Brighton
026	London - Bognor Regis
030	London - Fareham
203	Heathrow Airport - Portsmouth - Southsea
300	Bristol - Southsea

X4804	FJ11RDX	Volvo B9R	Caetano Levanté	C48FT	2011
X4805	FJ11RDY	Volvo B9R	Caetano Levanté	C48FT	2011
X4806	FJ61EWA	Volvo B9R	Caetano Levanté	C48FT	2011
X4807	FJ61EVW	Volvo B9R	Caetano Levanté	C48FT	2011
X4808	FN62CAO	Volvo B9R	Caetano Levanté	C48FT	2012
X4809	FN62CBV	Volvo B9R	Caetano Levanté	C48FT	2012
X4810	FN62CDX	Volvo B9R	Caetano Levanté	C48FT	2012
X4811	FN62CEY	Volvo B9R	Caetano Levanté	C48FT	2012
X4812	FN62CFG	Volvo B9R	Caetano Levanté	C48FT	2012
X4813	FN62CFX	Volvo B9R	Caetano Levanté	C48FT	2012
X4814	FN62CGE	Volvo B9R	Caetano Levanté	C48FT	2012
X4815	FN62CVS	Volvo B9R	Caetano Levanté	C48FT	2012
X4816	FN62CVY	Volvo B9R	Caetano Levanté	C48FT	2012
X4817	FN62CWD	Volvo B9R	Caetano Levanté	C48FT	2012
X4818	FN62CXP	Volvo B9R	Caetano Levanté	C48FT	2012
X4819	FN62CZP	Volvo B9R	Caetano Levanté	C48FT	2012
X4820	FN62CZZ	Volvo B9R	Caetano Levanté	C48FT	2012
X4821	BF63ZSD	Volvo B9R	Caetano Levanté	C48FT	2013
X4822	BF63ZSE	Volvo B9R	Caetano Levanté	C48FT	2013
X4823	BF63ZTC	Volvo B9R	Caetano Levanté	C48FT	2013
X4824	BF63ZTD	Volvo B9R	Caetano Levanté	C48FT	2013
X4825	BK15AHP	Scania K440 EB4	Caetano Levanté	C48FT	2015
X4826	BK15AHU	Scania K440 EB4	Caetano Levanté	C48FT	2015

Details of the vehicles in this fleet may be found in the *English Bus Handbook : Coaches* book

Displaying a representation of the British flag is Volvo B9R BF63ZTC from the 2013 delivery. It is seen in Portsmouth while heading for Fareham. *Dave Heath*

OXFORD BUS COMPANY

Oxford Bus Company, Cowley House, Watlington Rd, Oxford, OX4 6GA

737   Oxford - Stansted Airport

51	FJ60KVP	Volvo B9R	Caetano Levanté	C48FT	2010
52	FJ60KVR	Volvo B9R	Caetano Levanté	C48FT	2010
53	BX65WAO	Volvo B8R	Caetano Levanté	C48FT	2015
54	BX65WAU	Volvo B8R	Caetano Levanté	C48FT	2015
55	BX65WCK	Volvo B8R	Caetano Levanté	C48FT	2015

Details of the other vehicles in this fleet may be found in the annual *Go-Ahead Bus Handbook*.

PETER GODWARD COACHES

P Godward, 4 Edwin Hall View, South Woodham Ferrers, CM3 5QL

540   London - Manchester
550   London - Liverpool
560   London - Sheffield
561   London - Leeds

No vehicles are contracted in National Express colours. The vehicles used on the services are selected from the main fleet.

The Oxford Bus Company is a new contractor for National Express and are currently using three new coaches alongside five earlier vehicles. Seen on route 737 in Hemel Hempstead is 51, FJ60KVP.
Dave Heath

PARK'S OF HAMILTON

Parks of Hamilton (Coach Hirers) Ltd, 20 Bothwell Road, Hamilton, ML3 0AY

Walkham Park, Burrington Way, Plymouth, PL5 3LS

090	London - Southend-on-Sea
310	Bradford - Poole
315	Helston - Eastbourne
324	Huddersfield - Brixham
328	Plymouth - Blackpool
404	London - Penzance
406	London - Newquay
421	London - Blackpool
501	London - Plymouth - Totnes
504	London - Penzance
534	Glasgow - Hull
537	Glasgow - Corby
538	Inverness - Glasgow - Manchester Airport - Coventry
540	London - Rochdale - Burnley - Colne
561	London - Bradford
570	London - Blackpool
592	London - Glasgow - Aberdeen

SW09UMC	Volvo B12B 15m	Plaxton Panther	C65FT	2009
BSK723	Volvo B12B 15m	Plaxton Panther	C65FT	2009
NBW999	Volvo B9R 12.6m	Plaxton Elite	C48FT	2013
290WE	Volvo B9R 12.6m	Plaxton Elite	C48FT	2013
T4SCC	Volvo B9R 12.6m	Plaxton Elite	C48FT	2013
HSK642	Volvo B9R 12.6m	Plaxton Elite	C48FT	2011
HSK643	Volvo B9R 12.6m	Plaxton Elite	C48FT	2011
HSK644	Volvo B9R 12.6m	Plaxton Elite	C48FT	2011
HSK645	Volvo B9R 12.6m	Plaxton Elite	C48FT	2011
HSK646	Volvo B9R 12.6m	Plaxton Elite	C48FT	2011
KSK951	Volvo B9R 12.6m	Plaxton Elite	C48FT	2011
KSK952	Volvo B9R 12.6m	Plaxton Elite	C48FT	2011

Taunton is the location for this view of LSK812, a Volvo B13R with Plaxton Elite bodywork. *Steve Rice*

KSK953	Volvo B9R 12.6m	Plaxton Elite	C48FT	2011
KSK986	Volvo B9R 12.6m	Plaxton Elite	C48FT	2011
HSK651	Volvo B9R 12.6m	Plaxton Elite	C48FT	2012
HSK652	Volvo B9R 12.6m	Plaxton Elite	C48FT	2012
HSK653	Volvo B9R 12.6m	Plaxton Elite	C48FT	2012
HSK654	Volvo B9R 12.6m	Plaxton Elite	C48FT	2012
HSK655	Volvo B9R 12.6m	Plaxton Elite	C48FT	2012
HSK656	Volvo B9R 12.6m	Plaxton Elite	C48FT	2012
HSK657	Volvo B9R 12.6m	Plaxton Elite	C48FT	2012
HSK658	Volvo B9R 12.6m	Plaxton Elite	C48FT	2012
HSK659	Volvo B9R 12.6m	Plaxton Elite	C48FT	2012
HSK660	Volvo B9R 12.6m	Plaxton Elite	C48FT	2012
KSK984	Volvo B9R 12.6m	Plaxton Elite	C48FT	2012
KSK985	Volvo B9R 12.6m	Plaxton Elite	C48FT	2012
KSK978	Volvo B9R 12.6m	Plaxton Elite	C48FT	2013
LSK502	Volvo B9R 12.6m	Plaxton Elite	C48FT	2013
LSK807	Volvo B13R 15m	Plaxton Elite	C65FT	2014
LSK808	Volvo B13R 15m	Plaxton Elite	C65FT	2014
LSK812	Volvo B13R 15m	Plaxton Elite	C65FT	2014
LSK814	Volvo B13R 15m	Plaxton Elite	C65FT	2014
LSK815	Volvo B13R 15m	Plaxton Elite	C65FT	2014
LSK819	Volvo B13R 15m	Plaxton Elite	C65FT	2014
LSK825	Volvo B13R 15m	Plaxton Elite	C65FT	2014
LSK830	Volvo B13R 15m	Plaxton Elite	C65FT	2014
LSK831	Volvo B13R 15m	Plaxton Elite	C65FT	2014
LSK832	Volvo B13R 15m	Plaxton Elite	C65FT	2014
LSK835	Volvo B13R 15m	Plaxton Elite	C65FT	2014
LSK839	Volvo B13R 15m	Plaxton Elite	C65FT	2014
LSK845	Volvo B13R 15m	Plaxton Elite	C65FT	2014
LSK870	Volvo B13R 15m	Plaxton Elite	C65FT	2014

Previous registration:

BSK723	KSK949		
LSK807	YY63 WCJ	LSK830	YX14 SGO
LSK808	YY63 WCK	LSK832	YX14 SGV
LSK812	YY63 WCL	LSK835	YX14 SGY
LSK814	YY63 WCM	LSK839	YX14 SGZ
LSK815	YY63 WCN	LSK845	YX14 SHJ
LSK819	YY63 WCO	LSK870	YX14 SHV
LSK825	YY63 WCP	SW09UMC	KSK948

Depots: Plymouth and Hamilton. Details of the other vehicles in this fleet may be found in *The Scottish Bus Handbook*.

Comparison with the tri-axle on the previous page, Volvo B9R HSK656 is seen in Bristol while working route 328. *Mark Lyons*

SELWYNS

Hayton's - Selwyns

Selwyns Travel Ltd, Cavendish Farm Road, Weston, Runcorn, WA7 4LU

060	S/H	Liverpool - Manchester - Leeds
061	S/H	Leeds - Manchester Airport
304	S	Liverpool - Weymouth
323	S	Liverpool - Cardiff
325	H	Manchester - Birmingham
350	S	Liverpool - Clacton-on-Sea
381	S	Wrexham - Chester - Leeds
420	H	London - Birmingham
422	S	London - Burnley
440	H	London - Manchester
540	S	London - Manchester
540	H	London - Rochdale - Burnley
550	S	London - Liverpool - Birkenhead - Southport
580	S	Liverpool - Newcastle-upon-Tyne

131	S	FJ58AJU	Scania K340 EB4	Caetano Levanté	C49FT	2009
132	H	FJ58AJV	Scania K340 EB4	Caetano Levanté	C49FT	2009
139	S	FJ59APX	Scania K340 EB4	Caetano Levanté	C49FT	2009
140	S	FJ59APY	Scania K340 EB4	Caetano Levanté	C49FT	2009
141	S	YN10FKM	Volvo B9R	Plaxton Elite	C48FT	2010
142	S	YN10FKO	Volvo B9R	Plaxton Elite	C48FT	2010
143	S	YN10FKP	Volvo B9R	Plaxton Elite	C48FT	2010
144	S	YN10FKR	Volvo B9R	Plaxton Elite	C48FT	2010
145	S	YN10FKS	Volvo B9R	Plaxton Elite	C48FT	2010
146	S	YN10FKT	Volvo B9R	Plaxton Elite	C48FT	2010
147	S	YN10FKV	Volvo B9R	Plaxton Elite	C48FT	2010
153	S	YN11AYA	Volvo B9R	Plaxton Elite	C48FT	2011
154	S	YN11AYB	Volvo B9R	Plaxton Elite	C48FT	2011

Pictured while passing through Nottingham, Selwyn's 205, FN62CCZ, operates service 350 towards Liverpool. *Mark Lyons*

Illustrating the British flag on the rear of Caetano Levanté 170, FJ61EWZ, an example based at Hayton's depot near Manchester and pictured in that city. *Steve Rice*

155	S	YN11AYC	Volvo B9R	Plaxton Elite	C48FT	2011
156	S	YN11AYD	Volvo B9R	Plaxton Elite	C48FT	2011
161	H	FJ11MLV	Volvo B9R	Caetano Levanté	C48FT	2011
165	S	FJ61EWF	Volvo B9R	Caetano Levanté	C48FT	2011
166	S	FJ61EWG	Volvo B9R	Caetano Levanté	C48FT	2011
167	S	FJ61EWH	Volvo B9R	Caetano Levanté	C48FT	2011
168	S	FJ61EWK	Volvo B9R	Caetano Levanté	C48FT	2011
169	S	FJ61EWL	Volvo B9R	Caetano Levanté	C48FT	2011
170	S	FJ61EWM	Volvo B9R	Caetano Levanté	C48FT	2011
171	H	FJ61EWB	Volvo B9R	Caetano Levanté	C48FT	2011
172	H	FJ61EWZ	Volvo B9R	Caetano Levanté	C48FT	2011
173	H	FJ61EXK	Volvo B9R	Caetano Levanté	C48FT	2011
174	H	FJ61EXL	Volvo B9R	Caetano Levanté	C48FT	2011
186	H	FJ60EFU	Volvo B9R	Caetano Levanté	C48FT	2010
187	H	FJ60EFV	Volvo B9R	Caetano Levanté	C48FT	2010
188	S	FJ60EFW	Volvo B9R	Caetano Levanté	C48FT	2010
204	H	FN62CCV	Volvo B9R	Caetano Levanté	C48FT	2012
205	S	FN62CCZ	Volvo B9R	Caetano Levanté	C48FT	2012
206	S	FN62CDE	Volvo B9R	Caetano Levanté	C48FT	2012
207	S	FN62CDY	Volvo B9R	Caetano Levanté	C48FT	2012
208	S	FJ13DZZ	Volvo B9R	Caetano Levanté	C48FT	2013
209	S	FJ13EBC	Volvo B9R	Caetano Levanté	C48FT	2013
210	S	FJ13EBD	Volvo B9R	Caetano Levanté	C48FT	2013
211	S	FJ13EBF	Volvo B9R	Caetano Levanté	C48FT	2013

Details of the vehicles in this fleet may be found in our *English Bus Handbook : Coaches* book.

SILVERDALE

Silverdale Tours (Nottingham) Ltd, Little Tennis Street South, Nottingham, NG2 4EU

310	Leicester - Bradford
329	Nottingham - Newcastle-upon-Tyne
349	Nottingham - Stansted Airport
440	London - Leicester - Derby/Nottingham/Burton-upon-Trent
450	London - Nottingham
561	London - Bradford

FJ58AJO	Scania K340 EB4	Caetano Levanté	C49FT	2008
FJ09DWY	Scania K340 EB4	Caetano Levanté	C49FT	2009
FJ09DXT	Scania K340 EB4	Caetano Levanté	C49FT	2009
FJ09DXU	Scania K340 EB4	Caetano Levanté	C49FT	2009
FJ10EZT	Scania K340 EB4	Caetano Levanté	C49FT	2010
FJ10EZU	Scania K340 EB4	Caetano Levanté	C49FT	2010
FJ61EWP	Volvo B9R	Caetano Levanté	C48FT	2012
FJ61EWR	Volvo B9R	Caetano Levanté	C48FT	2012
FJ61EWT	Volvo B9R	Caetano Levanté	C48FT	2012
FJ61EWV	Volvo B9R	Caetano Levanté	C48FT	2012
FJ61EWW	Volvo B9R	Caetano Levanté	C48FT	2012
FJ61EYF	Volvo B9R	Caetano Levanté	C48FT	2012
BK15AHN	Scania K440 EB4	Caetano Levanté	C48FT	2015
BK15AHO	Scania K440 EB4	Caetano Levanté	C48FT	2015

Details of the vehicles in this fleet may be found in our *English Bus Handbook : Coaches* book

Newly into service Scania K440 BK15AHN is seen arriving in Nottingham on service 450 from London. Silverdale Tours has recently been acquired by Skills coach group. *Mark Lyons*

SKILLS MOTOR COACHES

Skills Motor Coaches Ltd, Belgrave Road, Bulwell, Nottingham, England, NG6 8LY

240	Bradford - Heathrow Airport
310	Bradford - Nottingham
387	Blackpool - Coventry
440	London - Leicester - Derby
461	London - Lichfield
675	Wolverhampton - Minehead (Butlins)

SV07ADO	Volvo B12B 15m	Plaxton Panther	C61FT	2007	Stagecoach, 2015
SV07ADU	Volvo B12B 15m	Plaxton Panther	C61FT	2007	Stagecoach, 2015
WX07OVJ	MAN 18.360	Plaxton Panther	C49FT	2007	MAN, Swindon, 2014
MIG9439	Scania K340 EB6	Caetano Levanté	C61FT	2007	National Express, 2015
MIG9440	Scania K340 EB6	Caetano Levanté	C61FT	2007	National Express, 2015
MIG9442	Scania K340 EB6	Caetano Levanté	C61FT	2007	National Express, 2015
SHZ5733	Scania K340 EB6	Caetano Levanté	C61FT	2007	National Express, 2015
SHZ5734	Scania K340 EB6	Caetano Levanté	C61FT	2008	National Express, 2015
SN10JJZ	Volvo B12BT	Plaxton Elite	C54FT	2010	Park's of Hamilton, 2015
SN10JKE	Volvo B12BT	Plaxton Elite	C54FT	2010	Park's of Hamilton, 2015
SN10JKF	Volvo B12BT	Plaxton Elite	C54FT	2010	Park's of Hamilton, 2015
SN10JRU	Volvo B12BT	Plaxton Elite	C54FT	2010	Park's of Hamilton, 2015
SW10VNS	Volvo B12BT	Plaxton Elite	C54FT	2010	Park's of Hamilton, 2015

Previous registrations:

MIG9439	FJ07DVR		SHZ5733	FJ57KJE
MIG9440	FJ07DVP		SHZ5734	FJ57KHF
MIG9442	FJ07DVK			

Details of the vehicles in this fleet may be found in our *English Bus Handbook : Coaches* book.

Acquired from Park's of Hamilton are five Volvo B9Rs with Plaxton Elite bodywork. Pictured while operating route 240, SN10JKF was passing through Chesterfield when pictured. *Tony Wilson*

SOUTH GLOUCESTERSHIRE

South Gloucestershire Bus & Coach, Pegasus Business Park, Gypsy Patch Lane,
Patchway, Bristol, BS34 6QD

040	London - Bristol - Burnham-on-Sea
200	Bristol - Gatwick Airport
302	Bristol - Northampton
318	Bristol - Birmingham
330	Nottingham - Penzance
339	Grimsby - Westward Ho!
401	London - Bristol
402	London - Frome
403	London - Bath
502	London - Ilfracombe
509	London - Cardiff

	NX53AAA	Scania K340 EB4	Caetano Levanté	C49FT	2007	National Express, 2015
SB1	T100SGB	Scania K340 EB6	Caetano Levanté	C61FT	2007	National Express, 2009
SB2	T200SGB	Scania K340 EB6	Caetano Levanté	C61FT	2007	National Express, 2009
SB3	T300SGB	Scania K340 EB6	Caetano Levanté	C61FT	2007	National Express, 2009
SB4	T400SGB	Scania K340 EB6	Caetano Levanté	C61FT	2008	
SB5	T500SGB	Scania K340 EB6	Caetano Levanté	C61FT	2008	
SB6	T600SGB	Scania K340 EB6	Caetano Levanté	C61FT	2008	
SB7	T700SGB	Scania K340 EB6	Caetano Levanté	C61FT	2008	
SB8	T800SGB	Scania K340 EB6	Caetano Levanté	C61FT	2008	
SB9	T900SGB	Scania K340 EB6	Caetano Levanté	C61FT	2008	
SB10	NX04AAA	Volvo B9R	Caetano Levanté	C48FT	2010	
SB11	NX54AAA	Volvo B9R	Caetano Levanté	C48FT	2010	
SB12	L400SGB	Volvo B9R	Caetano Levanté	C48FT	2010	
SB13	NX55AAA	Volvo B9R	Caetano Levanté	C48FT	2010	
SB14	NX59AAA	Volvo B9R	Caetano Levanté	C48FT	2010	
SB15	L80SGB	Volvo B9R	Caetano Levanté	C48FT	2010	
SB16	NX07AAA	Volvo B9R	Caetano Levanté	C48FT	2010	
SB17	NX57AAA	Volvo B9R	Caetano Levanté	C48FT	2010	
SB18	NX08AAA	Volvo B9R	Caetano Levanté	C48FT	2010	
SB19	NX58AAA	Volvo B9R	Caetano Levanté	C48FT	2010	
SB20	NX09AAA	Volvo B9R	Caetano Levanté	C48FT	2010	
SB21	L900SGB	Volvo B9R	Caetano Levanté	C48FT	2010	

**South Gloucestershire operates both Scania and Volvo products on National Express services.
Representing the tri-axle Scania coaches FJ59AKP, now registered T600SGB.** *Colin LLoyd*

Since the last edition of the National Express Coach Handbook most of the fleet have gained Select index marks. 2007 coach NX53AAA was latterly fleet number 3 with National Express. It was heading east from Bristol when seen at Heathrow airport. *Dave Heath*

SB22	NX10AAA	Volvo B9R	Caetano Levanté	C48FT	2012
SB23	NX60AAA	Volvo B9R	Caetano Levanté	C48FT	2012
SB24	NX11AAA	Volvo B9R	Caetano Levanté	C48FT	2012
SB25	NX61AAA	Volvo B9R	Caetano Levanté	C48FT	2012
SB36	NX12AAA	Volvo B9R	Caetano Levanté	C48FT	2012
SB37	FJ12FXG	Volvo B9R	Caetano Levanté	C48FT	2012
SB38	FJ12FXH	Volvo B9R	Caetano Levanté	C48FT	2012
SB39	FJ12FXL	Volvo B9R	Caetano Levanté	C48FT	2012
SB40	FJ12FXK	Volvo B9R	Caetano Levanté	C48FT	2012
SB26	BN64FKP	Volvo B8R	Caetano Levanté	C48FT	2014
SB27	BN64FKR	Volvo B8R	Caetano Levanté	C48FT	2014
SB28	BN64FKS	Volvo B8R	Caetano Levanté	C48FT	2014
SB29	BN64FKT	Volvo B8R	Caetano Levanté	C48FT	2014
SB30	BN64FKU	Volvo B8R	Caetano Levanté	C48FT	2014
SB31	BN64FKV	Volvo B8R	Caetano Levanté	C48FT	2014
SB32	BN64FKW	Volvo B8R	Caetano Levanté	C48FT	2014

Previous registrations:

L80SGB	FJ60HYU	NX58AAA	FJ60HYY
L400SGB	FJ60HYR	NX59AAA	FJ60HYT
L900SGB	FJ60HZA	NX60AAA	FJ61GZF
NX04AAA	FJ60HYC	NX61AAA	FJ61GZH
NX07AAA	FJ60HYV	T100SGB	FJ57KGF
NX08AAA	FJ60HYX	T200SGB	FJ57KGG
NX09AAA	FJ60HYZ	T300SGB	FJ57KHH
NX10AAA	FJ61GZE	T400SGB	FJ58AKN
NX11AAA	FJ61GZG	T500SGB	FJ58AKO
NX12AAA	FJ12FXF	T600SGB	FJ58AKP
NX53AAA	FJ57KHL	T700SGB	FJ58AKU
NX54AAA	FJ60HYF	T800SGB	FJ58AKV
NX55AAA	FJ60HYS	T900SGB	FJ58AKX
NX57AAA	FJ60HYW		

Details of the vehicles in this fleet may be found in our *English Bus Handbook: Coaches* book

STAGECOACH

Stagecoach UK operates several National Express services. Management units are based in Kent (SE) and Yorkshire (Y).

007	London - Dover - Deal	SE
021	London - Dover - Deal	SE
022	London - Ramsgate	SE
310	Sheffield - Leeds	Y
465	London - Huddersfield	Y
560	London - Barnsley	Y
564	London - Halifax	Y

Stagecoach vehicles allocated to National Express duties:

53701-53716		Volvo B9R			Plaxton Elite			C48FT	2010		
53701	SE	OU10GYH	53705	SE	OU10GYO	53709	SE	AE10JTV	53713	SE	YN60ACF
53702	SE	OU10GYJ	53706	SE	AE10JSZ	53710	SE	AE10JTX	53714	Y	YN60ACJ
53703	SE	OU10GYK	53707	SE	AE10JTO	53711	SE	AE10JTY	53715	Y	YN60ACO
53704	SE	OU10GYN	53708	SE	AE10JTU	53712	SE	YN60ABX	53716	Y	YN60ACU

53731-53738		Volvo B9R			Caetano Levante			C48FT	2013		
53731	Y	BF63ZRN	53733	Y	BF63ZRP	53735	Y	BF63ZRT	53737	Y	BF63ZRV
53732	Y	BF63ZRO	53734	Y	BF63ZRR	53736	Y	BF63ZRU	53738	Y	BF63ZRX

Details of the other vehicles in the Stagecoach fleet, along with allocation code details, may be found in the annual *Stagecoach Bus Handbook.*

E STOTT & SONS

E Stott & Sons Ltd, Colne Vale Garage, Saville Street, Milnsbridge, Huddersfield, HD3 4PG

310	Bradford - Leicester
320	Birmingham - Leeds
351	Sheffield - Blackpool
561	Bradford - London
660	Bradford - Skegness (Butlins)

FJ60EGD	Volvo B9R	Caetano Levanté	C48FT	2010
BK14LFE	Volvo B9R	Caetano Levanté	C48FT	2014
BK14LFF	Volvo B9R	Caetano Levanté	C48FT	2014

Details of the vehicles in this fleet may be found in the *English Bus Handbook: Notable Independents* book

Currently allocated to Dover for their National Express contracts, Volvo B9R 53710, AE10JTX illustrates the Plaxton Elite body supplied in 2010. *Mark Doggett*

STUART'S of CARLUKE

Stuarts Coaches Ltd, Castlehill, Airdrie Road, Carluke, ML8 5EP

544   Glasgow - London

FJ11MKO	Volvo B9R	Caetano Levanté	C48FT	2011
FJ11MKP	Volvo B9R	Caetano Levanté	C48FT	2011

Details of the other vehicles in this fleet may be found in *The Scottish Bus Handbook*.

TOWER TRANSIT

Whippet Coaches Ltd, 2 Rowles Way, Swavesey, CB24 4UG

010   London - Cambridge

NX08	BK15AHV	Volvo B8R	Caetano Levanté	C48FT	2015
NX09	BK15AHX	Volvo B8R	Caetano Levanté	C48FT	2015
NX10	BK15AHY	Volvo B8R	Caetano Levanté	C48FT	2015
NX11	BK15AJY	Volvo B8R	Caetano Levanté	C48FT	2015
NX12	BK15AKF	Volvo B8R	Caetano Levanté	C48FT	2015
NX13	BK15AKG	Volvo B8R	Caetano Levanté	C48FT	2015

Details of the vehicles in this fleet may be found in our *English Bus Handbook: Smaller Groups* book

TRAVELLERS CHOICE

Shaw Hadwin (John Shaw & Sons) Ltd, The Coach and Travel Centre, Scotland Road, Carnforth, LA5 9BQ

333   Blackpool - Bournemouth
341   Burnley - Birmingham - Paignton
570   London - Blackpool
571   London - Whitehaven

PO12GWG	Volvo B9R	Caetano Levanté	C48FT	2012
PO12GWJ	Volvo B9R	Caetano Levanté	C48FT	2012
PO12GWL	Volvo B9R	Caetano Levanté	C48FT	2012
PO12GWP	Volvo B9R	VDL Jonckheere	C53FT	2012
PO12GWW	Volvo B9R	VDL Jonckheere	C53FT	2012
PO62LMK	Volvo B9R	Caetano Levanté	C48FT	2013
PO62LNA	Volvo B9R	Caetano Levanté	C48FT	2013
FN63PXB	Volvo B11R	Caetano Levanté	C61FT	2014
PO65	Volvo B11R	Caetano Levanté	C61FT	2016
PO65	Volvo B11R	Caetano Levanté	C61FT	2016

Details of the other vehicles in this fleet may be found in the *English Bus Handbook : Coaches* book.

Tower Transit commenced operations in London in 2013 and in 2015 acquired the Cambridgeshire-based Whippet operation from where their National Express services operate. First of the new coaches, BK15AHV is shown. *Mark Doggett*

Recent changes have seen additional work for Travellers Choice. As we go to press two more coaches are expected in December for use on service 571 to Whitehaven. Representing the fleet is PO62LMK. *Dave Heath*

TRAVEL de COURCEY

Mike de Courcey Travel Ltd, Rowley Drive, Coventry CV3 4FG

210	Wolverhampton - Birmingham - Heathrow Airport - Gatwick Airport
310	Coventry - Birmingham - Leeds - Bradford
325	Birmingham - Manchester
410	London - Birmingham - Wolverhampton - Shewsbury
420	London - Birmingham - Wolverhampton
460	London - Stratford-upon-Avon - Coventry
540	London - Manchester
777	Birmingham - Stansted Airport

MD1-14 Volvo B9R Caetano Levanté C48FT 2011

MD1	FJ11MKZ	**MD5**	FJ11GME	**MD9**	FJ11GKZ	**MD12**	FJ11GKG
MD2	FJ11GKO	**MD6**	FJ11GKD	**MD10**	FJ11MLU	**MD13**	FJ11GKF
MD3	FJ11GMF	**MD7**	FJ11GKN	**MD11**	FJ11GMG	**MD14**	FJ11GKK
MD4	FJ11GKL	**MD8**	FJ11GJV				

MD15-28 Volvo B9R Caetano Levanté C48FT 2013

MD15	FN62CME	**MD19**	FJ13EAF	**MD23**	FJ13EAO	**MD26**	FJ13EAX
MD16	FN62CKY	**MD20**	FJ13EAG	**MD24**	FJ13EAP	**MD27**	FJ13EAY
MD17	FJ13EAA	**MD21**	FJ13EAK	**MD25**	FJ13EAW	**MD28**	FJ13EBA
MD18	FJ13EAC	**MD22**	FJ13EAM				

Details of the other vehicles in this fleet may be found in the *English Bus Handbook : Notable Independents* book.

London's Park Lane provides the location for this view of MD21, FJ13EAK, seen working an extention of route 420 to Shrewsbury. *Dave Heath*

TRAVELSTAR

Travelstar European Ltd, Marlow Street, Walsall, WS2 8AQ

210	Wolverhampton - Gatwick Airport
319	Oxford - Birmingham - Bradford
320	Birmingham - Bradford
460	Lonodn - Coventry
808	London - Wolverhampton

FJ11GOA	Volvo B9R	Caetano Levanté	C48FT	2011
FJ11GOC	Volvo B9R	Caetano Levanté	C48FT	2011
FJ61EVY	Volvo B9R	Caetano Levanté	C48FT	2012
FJ61GZA	Volvo B9R	Caetano Levanté	C48FT	2012
FJ61GZB	Volvo B9R	Caetano Levanté	C48FT	2012
BF63ZSR	Volvo B9R	Caetano Levanté	C48FT	2014

Seen departing Heathrow airport is BF63ZSR which joined Travelstar's fleet in 2014. *Dave Heath*

YELLOW BUSES - RATP

Bournemouth Transport Ltd, Yeoman's Way, Bournemouth, BH8 0BQ

032   London - Southampton
035   London - Poole - Weymouth

330-337		Volvo B9R		Caetano Levanté		C49FT		2010-12	
330	FJ60HYN	332	FJ61EWC	334	FJ61EWE			336	FJ61GZM
331	FJ60HYO	333	FJ61EWD	335	FJ61GZL			337	FJ61GZN

338	FJ12FXE	Volvo B9R		Caetano Levanté	C48FT	2012
339	FJ12FXT	Volvo B9R		Caetano Levanté	C48FT	2012
340	FJ13DZX	Volvo B9R		Caetano Levanté	C48FT	2013
341	FJ13DZY	Volvo B9R		Caetano Levanté	C48FT	2013

342-347		Volvo B8R		Caetano Levanté		C49FT		2014-15	
342	BK14LFG	344	BK14LFJ	346	BK15AHZ			347	BK15AJO
343	BK14LFH	345	BK14LFL						

Details of the other vehicles in this RATP fleet may be found in the *English Bus Handbook : Groups* book.

2014 saw six coaches joining the RATP groups Bournemouth operation where they displaced older coaches from the network. Volvo B8R 345, BK14LFL is seen leaving its home town for London.
Steve Rice

YEOMANS

Yeomans Canyon Travel Ltd, 21-23 Three Elms Trading Estate, Hereford, HR4 9PU

| 444 | London - Hereford |
| 445 | London - Hereford |

45	FJ60EFZ	Volvo B9R	Caetano Levanté	C48FT	2010
46	FJ60HYG	Volvo B9R	Caetano Levanté	C48FT	2010
	BK15AKJ	Scania K440 EB4	Caetano Levanté	C48FT	2015
	BK15AKO	Scania K440 EB4	Caetano Levanté	C48FT	2015
	BK15AKN	Scania K440 EB4	Caetano Levanté	C48FT	2015

Details of other vehicles in this fleet may be found in the *English Bus Handbook : Notable Independents* book.

Yeomans have recently received three new Scania coaches with two on the 2010 Volvo B9Rs currently in use. One of these, FJ60EFZ is shown. *Terry Longhurst*

Index to National Express routes

007	London - Dover	Stagecoach
010	London - Cambridge	Tower Transit (Cambridge)
021	London - Dover	Stagecoach
022	London - Ramsgate	Stagecoach
023	London - Bexhill	Chalfont
024	London - Eastbourne	Go-Ahead Northern
025	London - Brighton	Lucketts
026	London - Bognor Regis	Lucketts
030	London - Fareham/Southsea	Lucketts
031	London - Portsmouth	East Yorkshire
032	London - Bournemouth/Southampton	Yellow Buses
033	London - Salisbury - Yeovil	Go-Ahead South Coast
035	London - Poole/Bournemouth	Yellow Buses
035	London - Bournemouth	Chalfont (Harrow)
035	London - Bournemouth University	Go-Ahead South Coast
040	London - Bristol - Burnham-on-Sea	South Gloucestershire
060	Leeds - Manchester- Liverpool	Selwyns / Hayton's
061	Leeds - Manchester Airport	Selwyns / Hayton's
090	London - Southend-on-Sea	Park's of Hamilton
200	Gatwick Airport - Bristol	South Gloucestershire
201	Gatwick Airport - Swansea	Edwards Coaches
202	Heathrow Airport - Cardiff	Edwards Coaches
203	Heathrow Airport - Southsea	Lucketts
205	Heathrow Airport - Poole	Go South Coast
206	Gatwick Airport - Poole	Go South Coast
210	Gatwick - Heathrow - Wolverhampton - Birmingham	Travel de Courcey
210	Gatwick - Heathrow - Wolverhampton - Birmingham	Travelstar
216	Cardiff - Bristol Airport	Edwards Coaches
230	Gatwick Airport - Nottingham - Derby	Chalfont (Northampton)
240	Heathrow Airport - Bradford	Skills
250	Heathrow Airport - Ipswich	Galloway
300	Bristol - Southsea	Lucketts
302	Bristol - Northampton	South Gloucestershire
304	Liverpool - Birmingham - Weymouth	Selwyns
310	Bradford - Leicester	E Scott
310	Bradford - Poole	Park's of Hamilton
310	Bradford - Leicester	Silverdale
310	Bradford - Nottingham	Skills
310	Sheffield - Leeds	Stagecoach
310	Coventry - Birmingham - Bradford	Travel de Courcey
315	Eastbourne - Helston	Park's of Hamilton
318	Birmingham - Bristol	South Gloucestershire
319	Bradford - Oxford	Travelstar
320	Leeds - Birmingham	E Scott
320	Bradford - Birmingham - Cardiff	Edwards
320	Bradford - Birmingham	Travelstar
321	Bradford - Birmingham	Edwards
322	Hull - Birmingham - Swansea	East Yorkshire
322	Birmingham - Swansea	Edwards
323	Liverpool - Cardiff	Selwyns / Hayton's
324	Bradford - Paignton	Park's of Hamilton
325	Birmingham - Manchester	Selwyns / Hayton's
325	Birmingham - Manchester	Travel de Courcey
327	Scarborough - Bristol	East Yorkshire

Park's SW09UMC is one of two Plaxton Panthers still operating for National Express while we show another view of Yellow Buses' BK14LFL heading for London. *Steve Rice*

328	Rochdale - Manchester - Plymouth	Park's of Hamilton
329	Nottingham - Newcastle-upon-Tyne	Silverdale
330	Nottingham - Penzance	South Gloucestershire
332	Newcastle-upon-Tyne - Swindon	Go North East
333	Blackpool - Bournemouth	Traveller's Choice
336	Edinburgh - Plymouth	Bruce's Coaches
337	Rugby - Brixham	South Glocestershire
339	Grimsby - Westward Ho!	South Glocestershire
341	Burnley - Birmingham - Southsea	Traveller's Choice
343	Birmingham - Swansea	Edwards
349	Nottingham - Stansted Airport	Johnson Bros
349	Nottingham - Stansted Airport	Silverdale
350	Liverpool - Stansted Airport	Johnson Bros
350	Liverpool - Stansted - Clacton-on-Sea	Selwyns / Hayton's
351	Blackpool - Leeds	E Stott
370	Runcorn - Clacton-on-Sea	Selwyns / Hayton's
371	Birmingham - Great Yarmouth	Ambassador Travel
380	Newcastle-upon-Tyne - Leeds - Liverpool	Go North East
381	Leeds - Chester - Wrexham	Selwyn's
385	Manchester - Bangor	Llew Jones
387	Blackpool - Coventry	Skills
397	Blackpool - Leicester	Hamiltons
401	London - Bath	South Gloucestershire
402	London - Frome	South Gloucestershire
403	London - Bath	South Gloucestershire
404	London - Penzance	Park's of Hamilton
406	London - Newquay	Park's of Hamilton
409	London - Aberystwyth	NX West Midlands
410	London - Birmingham - Wolverhampton	Epsom Coaches
410	London - Birmingham	Go North East
410	London - Birmingham - Wolverhampton	Travel de Courcey
410	London - Birmingham - Wolverhampton	Whittle
420	London - Birmingham	Go North East
420	London - Birmingham	Selwyns / Hayton's
420	London - Birmingham - Wolverhampton	Travel de Courcey
421	London - Blackpool	Park's of Hamilton
422	London - Burnley	Selwyns / Hayton's
425	London - Newcastle-upon-Tyne	Go North East
425	London - Newcastle-upon-Tyne - Ashington	Jim Hughes
426	London - Sunderland - South Shields	Go North East
426	London - Sunderland - South Shields	Jim Hughes
435	London - Ashington	Jim Hughes
436	London - South Shields	Jim Hughes
440	London - Leicester - Manchester	Chalfont (Harrow)
440	London - Leicester - Manchester	Selwyns / Hayton's
440	London - Leicester - Burton upon Trent	Silverdale
440	London - Leicester - Derby	Skills
444	London - Gloucester	Bennetts
444	London - Gloucester - Worcester	NX West Midlands
444	London - Gloucester - Worcester	Yeomans
445	London - Hereford	Yeomans
447	London - Hull	East Yorkshire
448	London - Peterborough - Grimsby	East Yorkshire
449	London - Mablethorpe	East Yorkshire
450	London - Nottingham - Mansfield - Retford	Silverdale
450	London - Nottingham	Chalfont (Northampton)
455	London - Northampton	Chalfont (Northampton)
460	London - Straftord-upon-Avon - Coventry	Chalfont (Harrow)
460	London - Straftord-upon-Avon - Coventry	Travel de Courcey

Route 530 and Go-Ahead's 7096, FJ08KLU, leaves England's south west coast for Newcastle. *Steve Rice*

460	London - Strafford-upon-Avon - Coventry	Travelstar
461	London - Lichfield	Skills
465	London - Huddersfield	Stagecoach
481	London - Ipswich - Felixstowe	Galloway European
484	London - Walton-on-the-Naze	East Yorkshire
490	London - Norwich - Great Yarmouth	Chenery
490	London - Norwich (university of East Englia)	Ambassador Travel
491	London - Lowestoft	Ambassador Travel
497	London - Great Yarmouth	Ambassador Travel
498	London - Long Stratton	Chenery
501	London - Totnes - Brixham	Park's of Hamilton
502	London - Ilfracombe	South Gloucestershire
504	London - Penzance	NX Sipson Road
504	London - Penzance	Park's of Hamilton
507	London - Swansea	Edwards Coaches
508	London - Haverfordwest	Edwards Coaches
509	London - Cardiff	Chalfont
509	London - Cardiff	Edwards Coaches
509	London - Cardiff	South Gloucestershire
528	Rochdale - Birmingham - Haverfordwest	Edwards Coaches
530	Newcastle-upon-Tyne - Paignton	Go North East
531	Newcastle-upon-Tyne - Plymouth	Go North East
532	Edinburgh - Plymouth	Bruce's
534	Glasgow - Hull	Park's of Hmailton
537	Glasgow - Corby	Park's of Hamilton
538	Inverness - Manchester - Chester	Park's of Hamilton

The National Express Handbook

Ulsterbus operates four coaches in National Express livery on EuroLines services which pass through the UK; EuroLines routes being numbered 9xx. Plaxton-bodied Volvo 122, KEZ9122, is pictured in Preston while operating EuroLines 921 to Birmingham. *Steve Rice*

538	Aberdeen - Manchester - Chester	Park's of Hamilton
538	Inverness - Birmingham	Park's of Hamilton
539	Edinburgh - Bournemouth	Bruce's
540	London - Liverpool	Epsom Coaches
540	London - Burnley / Rochdale	Selwyns / Hayton's
540	London - Rochdale/Colne	Park's of Hamilton
540	London - Manchester	Peter Godward
540	London - Manchester / Liverpool	Travel de Courcey
544	Glasgow - London	Stuarts Coaches
545	London - Llandudno - Pwllheli	NX West Midlands
550	London - Liverpool	Peter Godward
550	London - Birkenhead - Liverpool	Selwyns / Hayton's
560	London - Sheffield	Peter Godward
560	London - Sheffield - Barnsley	Stagecoach
561	London - Bradford	Abbott
561	London - Bradford	BL Travel
561	London - Bradford	E Stott
561	London - Bradford	Excalibur
561	London - Skipton	Go North East
561	London - Bradford	Johnon Bros (Worksop)
561	London - Bradford	NX Sipson Road
561	London - Bradford	Parks of Hamilton

561	London - Bradford	Peter Godward
561	London - Bradford	Silverdale
562	London - Hull	East Yorkshire
563	London - Whitby	East Yorkshire
564	London - Halifax	Stagecoach
570	London - Blackpool	Traveller's Choice
570	London - Blackpool	Park's of Hamilton
571	London - Whitehaven	Traveller's Choice
580	Liverpool - Newcastle-upon-Tyne	Go North East
580	Liverpool - Newcastle-upon-Tyne	Selwyns
588	London - Inverness	Bruce's
590	London - Glasgow - Aberdeen	Bruce's
591	London - Edinburgh	Go North East
592	London - Glasgow - Aberdeen	Park's of Hamilton
594	London - Edinburgh	Go North East
660	Bradford - Skegness (Butlins)	Stott
661	Coventry - Skegness (Butlins)	Chalfont (Northampton)
662	Birmingham - Skegness (Butlins)	-
663	Newcastle upon Tyne - Skegness (Butlins)	Go North East
672	Swansea - Minehead (Butlins)	Edwards Coaches
675	Wolverhampton - Minehead (Butlins)	Skills
701	Heathrow Airport - Woking	National Express
702	Heathrow Airport - Aldershot	National Express
707	Gatwick Airport - Northampton	Chalfont (Northampton)
727	Brighton - Gatwick Airport - Norwich	National Express
737	Stansted Airport - Oxford	Oxford Bus Company
747	Brighton - Gatwick - Heathrow Airport	National Express
777	Stansted Airport - Birmingham	Travel de Courcey
787	Cambridge - Heathrow	National Express
801	London - Bradford	Epsom Coaches
802	London - Liverpool	Epsom Coaches
803	London - Gloucester	Bennetts
805	London - Plymouth	Park's of Hamilton
806	London - Poole	Go South Coast
808	London - Wolverhampton	Epsom Coaches
808	London - Wolverhampton	Travelstar
813	London - Norwich	Chenery
A1	London - Luton Airport	National Express
A3	London - Gatwick Airport	National Express
A6	London - Stansted Airport	National Express
A8	London - Stansted Airport	National Express
A9	London (Liverpool St) - Stansted Airport	National Express

Edwards FJ60HXX heads for Bristol Airport on service 215 while Bruce's FJ14GPV was pictured in Exeter as it headed home one September afternoon. *Steve Rice*

Vehicle Index

290 WE	Park's of Hamilton	BK14LFT	National Express	BX65WAE	National Express WM
574CPT	Go North East	BK14LFU	National Express	BX65WAJ	National Express WM
AE10JSZ	Stagecoach	BK14LFV	National Express	BX65WAO	Oxford Bus Company
AE10JTO	Stagecoach	BK14LFW	National Express	BX65WOU	Oxford Bus Company
AE10JTU	Stagecoach	BK14LFX	National Express	FH06EBM	Jim Hughes
AE10JTV	Stagecoach	BK14LFY	National Express	FJ06GGK	R W Chenery
AE10JTX	Stagecoach	BK14LGA	National Express	FJ07DVO	National Express
AE10JTY	Stagecoach	BK14LGC	National Express	FJ08KLF	Go North East
BF63 ZTC	Lucketts Travel	BK14LGD	National Express	FJ08KLS	Go North East
BF63 ZTD	Lucketts Travel	BK14LGE	National Express	FJ08KLU	Go North East
BF63ZPV	Go North East	BK14LGF	National Express	FJ08KLX	Go North East
BF63ZPW	Go North East	BK14LGG	National Express	FJ08KLZ	Go North East
BF63ZPY	Go North East	BK14LGJ	National Express	FJ08KMU	Go North East
BF63ZPZ	Go North East	BK14LGL	National Express	FJ08KMV	Go North East
BF63ZRA	Go North East	BK14LGN	National Express	FJ08KNV	Go North East
BF63ZRC	Go North East	BK14LGO	National Express	FJ08KNW	Go North East
BF63ZRL	Bennetts of Gloucester	BK14LGU	National Express	FJ09DWY	Silverdale Tours
BF63ZRN	Stagecoach	BK14LGV	National Express	FJ09DXA	Ambassador
BF63ZRO	Stagecoach	BK14LGW	National Express	FJ09DXB	Ambassador
BF63ZRP	Stagecoach	BK14LKZ	National Express	FJ09DXC	Ambassador
BF63ZRR	Stagecoach	BK15AHN	Silverdale Tours	FJ09DXE	Ambassador
BF63ZRT	Stagecoach	BK15AHO	Silverdale Tours	FJ09DXT	Silverdale Tours
BF63ZRU	Stagecoach	BK15AHP	Lucketts Travel	FJ09DXU	Silverdale Tours
BF63ZRV	Stagecoach	BK15AHU	Lucketts Travel	FJ10EZT	Silverdale Tours
BF63ZRX	Stagecoach	BK15AHV	Tower Transit	FJ10EZU	Silverdale Tours
BF63ZRY	Go North East	BK15AHX	Tower Transit	FJ10EZV	National Express
BF63ZRZ	Go North East	BK15AHY	Tower Transit	FJ11GJO	National Express
BF63ZSD	Lucketts Travel	BK15AHZ	Yellow Buses	FJ11GJU	National Express
BF63ZSE	Lucketts Travel	BK15AJO	Yellow Buses	FJ11GJV	Travel DeCourcey
BF63ZSG	Chalfont (Southall)	BK15AJU	National Express WM	FJ11GJX	National Express WM
BF63ZSJ	Chalfont (Southall)	BK15AJV	National Express WM	FJ11GJY	National Express WM
BF63ZSK	Ambassador	BK15AJX	Galloway	FJ11GJZ	National Express WM
BF63ZSL	Ambassador	BK15AJY	Tower Transit	FJ11GKA	National Express WM
BF63ZSN	Ambassador	BK15AKF	Tower Transit	FJ11GKC	National Express WM
BF63ZSO	Go South Coast	BK15AKG	Tower Transit	FJ11GKD	Travel DeCourcey
BF63ZSP	Go South Coast	BK15AKJ	Yeomans	FJ11GKF	Travel DeCourcey
BF63ZSR	Travelstar European	BK15AKN	Yeomans	FJ11GKG	Travel DeCourcey
BK14LDV	Bennetts of Gloucester	BK15AKO	Yeomans	FJ11GKK	Travel DeCourcey
BK14LDX	Bennetts of Gloucester	BL14LSO	Excalibur	FJ11GKL	Travel DeCourcey
BK14LDY	Bennetts of Gloucester	BL14LSU	Excalibur	FJ11GKN	Travel DeCourcey
BK14LDZ	Bennetts of Gloucester	BL14LSV	Excalibur	FJ11GKO	Travel DeCourcey
BK14LEF	Chalfont (Northampton)	BL14LSX	Excalibur	FJ11GKP	National Express
BK14LEJ	Chalfont (Northampton)	BN64FKL	National Express	FJ11GKU	National Express
BK14LEU	Chalfont (Northampton)	BN64FKM	National Express	FJ11GKV	National Express
BK14LFA	Chalfont (Northampton)	BN64FKO	National Express	FJ11GKX	National Express
BK14LFB	Chalfont (Northampton)	BN64FKP	South Gloucestershire	FJ11GKY	Edwards Coaches
BK14LFD	Chalfont (Northampton)	BN64FKR	South Gloucestershire	FJ11GKZ	Travel DeCourcey
BK14LFE	Stotts	BN64FKS	South Gloucestershire	FJ11GLF	Epsom Coaches
BK14LFF	Stotts	BN64FKT	South Gloucestershire	FJ11GLK	National Express
BK14LFG	Yellow Buses	BN64FKU	South Gloucestershire	FJ11GLV	National Express WM
BK14LFH	Yellow Buses	BN64FKV	South Gloucestershire	FJ11GLZ	National Express
BK14LFJ	Yellow Buses	BN64FKW	South Gloucestershire	FJ11GME	Travel DeCourcey
BK14LFL	Yellow Buses	BN64FKY	Edwards Coaches	FJ11GMF	Travel DeCourcey
BK14LFP	National Express	BN64FKZ	Edwards Coaches	FJ11GMG	Travel DeCourcey
BK14LFR	National Express	BSK723	Park's of Hamilton	FJ11GMO	Edwards Coaches
BK14LFS	National Express	BX65WAA	National Express WM	FJ11GMU	Edwards Coaches

Motorways are essential for the National Express network. National Express 137, FJ12FYM, passes Go Northern's 4024, FJ11MMK, as they both head north. *Terry O'Neil*

FJ11GMV	Epsom Coaches	FJ11MKG	National Express	FJ12FXH	South Gloucestershire
FJ11GMX	Edwards Coaches	FJ11MKK	National Express	FJ12FXK	South Gloucestershire
FJ11GMY	Edwards Coaches	FJ11MKL	National Express	FJ12FXL	South Gloucestershire
FJ11GMZ	Edwards Coaches	FJ11MKM	National Express	FJ12FXM	Edwards Coaches
FJ11GNF	Edwards Coaches	FJ11MKN	National Express	FJ12FXO	Edwards Coaches
FJ11GNK	Edwards Coaches	FJ11MKO	Stuarts Carluke	FJ12FXP	Edwards Coaches
FJ11GNN	Edwards Coaches	FJ11MKP	Stuarts Carluke	FJ12FXR	Edwards Coaches
FJ11GNO	Edwards Coaches	FJ11MKU	National Express	FJ12FXS	Edwards Coaches
FJ11GNP	Go South Coast	FJ11MKV	National Express	FJ12FXT	Yellow Buses
FJ11GNU	Go South Coast	FJ11MKZ	Travel DeCourcey	FJ12FXU	Edwards Coaches
FJ11GNV	Go South Coast	FJ11MLE	National Express	FJ12FXV	Edwards Coaches
FJ11GNX	Go South Coast	FJ11MLF	National Express	FJ12FXW	Edwards Coaches
FJ11GNY	Go South Coast	FJ11MLK	National Express	FJ12FXX	Edwards Coaches
FJ11GNZ	Go South Coast	FJ11MLL	National Express	FJ12FXY	Edwards Coaches
FJ11GOA	Travelstar European	FJ11MLN	National Express	FJ12FXZ	Edwards Coaches
FJ11GOC	Travelstar European	FJ11MLO	National Express	FJ12FYA	Edwards Coaches
FJ11GOH	Edwards Coaches	FJ11MLU	Travel DeCourcey	FJ12FYB	Edwards Coaches
FJ11MJK	National Express	FJ11MLV	Selwyns / Haytons	FJ12FYC	Edwards Coaches
FJ11MJO	National Express	FJ11RDO	National Express	FJ12FYD	Edwards Coaches
FJ11MJU	National Express	FJ11RDU	National Express	FJ12FYE	Edwards Coaches
FJ11MJV	National Express	FJ11RDV	National Express	FJ12FYF	Edwards Coaches
FJ11MJX	National Express	FJ11RDX	Lucketts Travel	FJ12FYG	Edwards Coaches
FJ11MJY	National Express	FJ11RDY	Lucketts Travel	FJ12FYH	National Express
FJ11MKA	R W Chenery	FJ12FXA	Johnson Bros	FJ12FYK	Edwards Coaches
FJ11MKC	R W Chenery	FJ12FXC	Edwards Coaches	FJ12FYL	National Express
FJ11MKD	National Express	FJ12FXD	National Express	FJ12FYM	National Express
FJ11MKE	National Express	FJ12FXE	Yellow Buses	FJ12FYN	National Express
FJ11MKF	National Express	FJ12FXG	South Gloucestershire	FJ12FYO	National Express

The National Express Handbook

Parliament Square provides a background to Galloway's FN62CAA as works its Felixstow service.
Dave Heath

FJ12FYP	National Express	FJ13ECC	National Express	FJ60HXS	R W Chenery
FJ12FYR	National Express	FJ13ECF	National Express	FJ60HXT	Oxford Bus Company
FJ13DZX	Yellow Buses	FJ13ECO	National Express	FJ60HXU	Oxford Bus Company
FJ13DZY	Yellow Buses	FJ13ECT	National Express	FJ60HXV	Edwards Coaches
FJ13DZZ	Selwyns / Haytons	FJ14GPV	Bruce's	FJ60HXW	Go North East
FJ13EAA	Travel DeCourcey	FJ57KHA	National Express	FJ60HXX	Edwards Coaches
FJ13EAC	Travel DeCourcey	FJ57KHG	National Express	FJ60HXY	National Express
FJ13EAF	Travel DeCourcey	FJ57KHP	Jim Hughes	FJ60HYB	Go North East
FJ13EAG	Travel DeCourcey	FJ57KHR	Jim Hughes	FJ60HYG	Yeomans
FJ13EAK	Travel DeCourcey	FJ57KHT	National Express	FJ60HYN	Yellow Buses
FJ13EAM	Travel DeCourcey	FJ58AJO	Silverdale Tours	FJ60HYO	Yellow Buses
FJ13EAO	Travel DeCourcey	FJ58AJU	Selwyns / Haytons	FJ60KVM	Go North East
FJ13EAP	Travel DeCourcey	FJ58AJV	Selwyns / Haytons	FJ60KVO	Go North East
FJ13EAW	Travel DeCourcey	FJ59APX	Selwyns / Haytons	FJ60KVP	Oxford Bus Company
FJ13EAX	Travel DeCourcey	FJ59APY	Selwyns / Haytons	FJ60KVR	Oxford Bus Company
FJ13EAY	Travel DeCourcey	FJ60EFU	Selwyns / Haytons	FJ60KVS	Oxford Bus Company
FJ13EBA	Travel DeCourcey	FJ60EFV	Selwyns / Haytons	FJ61EVN	Galloway
FJ13EBC	Selwyns / Haytons	FJ60EFW	Selwyns / Haytons	FJ61EVP	Galloway
FJ13EBD	Selwyns / Haytons	FJ60EFZ	Yeomans	FJ61EVR	Galloway
FJ13EBF	Selwyns / Haytons	FJ60EGD	Stotts	FJ61EVU	Galloway
FJ13EBK	National Express	FJ60EGE	Johnson Bros	FJ61EVV	Galloway
FJ13EBL	National Express	FJ60EGF	Johnson Bros	FJ61EVW	Lucketts Travel
FJ13EBM	National Express	FJ60EGY	Go North East	FJ61EVY	Travelstar European
FJ13EBO	National Express	FJ60EHB	Go South Coast	FJ61EWA	Lucketts Travel
FJ13EBP	National Express	FJ60EHC	Go South Coast	FJ61EWB	Selwyns / Haytons
FJ13EBU	National Express	FJ60EHD	Go South Coast	FJ61EWC	Yellow Buses
FJ13EBV	National Express	FJ60EHE	Go South Coast	FJ61EWD	Yellow Buses
FJ13ECA	National Express	FJ60EHF	Go South Coast	FJ61EWE	Yellow Buses

Tri-axle Volvo B13R LSK845 sets out along Park Lane in London as head for Blackpool. *Dave Heath*

FJ61EWF	Selwyns / Haytons	FJ61GZN	Yellow Buses	FN63PWJ	Bruce's
FJ61EWG	Selwyns / Haytons	FN06FMA	Jim Hughes	FN63PWK	Bruce's
FJ61EWH	Selwyns / Haytons	FN07BYV	National Express	FN63PWL	Bruce's
FJ61EWK	Selwyns / Haytons	FN07BZA	National Express	FN63PWO	Bruce's
FJ61EWL	Selwyns / Haytons	FN07BZC	National Express	FN63PWU	Bruce's
FJ61EWM	Selwyns / Haytons	FN62CAA	Galloway	FN63PWX	Bruce's
FJ61EWN	Chalfont (Southall)	FN62CAO	Lucketts Travel	FN63PWY	Bruce's
FJ61EWO	Chalfont (Southall)	FN62CBV	Lucketts Travel	FN63PWZ	Bruce's
FJ61EWP	Silverdale Tours	FN62CCV	Selwyns / Haytons	FN63PXB	Travellers Choice
FJ61EWR	Silverdale Tours	FN62CCZ	Selwyns / Haytons	HSK642	Park's of Hamilton
FJ61EWT	Silverdale Tours	FN62CDE	Selwyns / Haytons	HSK643	Park's of Hamilton
FJ61EWV	Silverdale Tours	FN62CDX	Lucketts Travel	HSK644	Park's of Hamilton
FJ61EWW	Silverdale Tours	FN62CDY	Selwyns / Haytons	HSK645	Park's of Hamilton
FJ61EWX	Go South Coast	FN62CEA	East Yorkshire	HSK646	Park's of Hamilton
FJ61EWY	Go South Coast	FN62CEU	East Yorkshire	HSK651	Park's of Hamilton
FJ61EWZ	Selwyns / Haytons	FN62CEY	Lucketts Travel	HSK652	Park's of Hamilton
FJ61EXK	Selwyns / Haytons	FN62CFG	Lucketts Travel	HSK653	Park's of Hamilton
FJ61EXL	Selwyns / Haytons	FN62CFX	Lucketts Travel	HSK654	Park's of Hamilton
FJ61EXT	Excalibur	FN62CGE	Lucketts Travel	HSK655	Park's of Hamilton
FJ61EXX	Excalibur	FN62CGX	East Yorkshire	HSK656	Park's of Hamilton
FJ61EYF	Silverdale Tours	FN62CKY	Travel DeCourcey	HSK657	Park's of Hamilton
FJ61EYG	Galloway	FN62CME	Travel DeCourcey	HSK658	Park's of Hamilton
FJ61EYK	Epsom Coaches	FN62CVS	Lucketts Travel	HSK659	Park's of Hamilton
FJ61EYL	Epsom Coaches	FN62CVY	Lucketts Travel	HSK660	Park's of Hamilton
FJ61GZA	Travelstar European	FN62CWD	Lucketts Travel	JCN822	Go North East
FJ61GZB	Travelstar European	FN62CXP	Lucketts Travel	KSK950	Park's of Hamilton
FJ61GZL	Yellow Buses	FN62CZP	Lucketts Travel	KSK951	Park's of Hamilton
FJ61GZM	Yellow Buses	FN62CZZ	Lucketts Travel	KSK952	Park's of Hamilton

The National Express Handbook

National Express's own 191, BK14LGG, is seen on Finchley Road in London's St John's Wood as it works Service A6. The A6 service which links the capital with Stansted airport has a frequency of every 15 minutes during the day. *Mark Lyons*

KSK953	Park's of Hamilton	MIG9438	National Express	PO12GWL	Travellers Choice
KSK978	Park's of Hamilton	MIG9439	Skills	PO12GWP	Travellers Choice
KSK982	Park's of Hamilton	MIG9440	Skills	PO12GWW	Travellers Choice
KSK983	Park's of Hamilton	MIG9442	Skills	PO62LMK	Travellers Choice
KSK984	Park's of Hamilton	MIG9443	National Express	PO62LNA	Travellers Choice
KSK985	Park's of Hamilton	NBW999	Park's of Hamilton	SHZ5733	Skills
KSK986	Park's of Hamilton	NX04AAA	South Gloucestershire	SHZ5734	Skills
L400SGB	South Gloucestershire	NX07AAA	South Gloucestershire	SHZ5735	National Express
L80SGB	South Gloucestershire	NX08AAA	South Gloucestershire	SN10JJZ	Skills
L900SGB	South Gloucestershire	NX09AAA	South Gloucestershire	SN10JKE	Skills
LJ12LLJ	Llew Jones	NX10AAA	South Gloucestershire	SN10JKF	Skills
LSK 502	Park's of Hamilton	NX11AAA	South Gloucestershire	SN10JRU	Skills
LSK507	Park's of Hamilton	NX12AAA	South Gloucestershire	SV07ADO	Skills
LSK807	Park's of Hamilton	NX53AAA	South Gloucestershire	SV07ADU	Skills
LSK808	Park's of Hamilton	NX54AAA	South Gloucestershire	SW09UMC	Park's of Hamilton
LSK812	Park's of Hamilton	NX55AAA	South Gloucestershire	SW10VNS	Skills
LSK814	Park's of Hamilton	NX57AAA	South Gloucestershire	T100SGB	South Gloucestershire
LSK815	Park's of Hamilton	NX58AAA	South Gloucestershire	T200SGB	South Gloucestershire
LSK819	Park's of Hamilton	NX59AAA	South Gloucestershire	T300SGB	South Gloucestershire
LSK825	Park's of Hamilton	NX60AAA	South Gloucestershire	T4 SCC	Park's of Hamilton
LSK830	Park's of Hamilton	NX61AAA	South Gloucestershire	T400SGB	South Gloucestershire
LSK831	Park's of Hamilton	OU10GYH	Stagecoach	T500SGB	South Gloucestershire
LSK832	Park's of Hamilton	OU10GYJ	Stagecoach	T600SGB	South Gloucestershire
LSK835	Park's of Hamilton	OU10GYK	Stagecoach	T700SGB	South Gloucestershire
LSK839	Park's of Hamilton	OU10GYN	Stagecoach	T800SGB	South Gloucestershire
LSK845	Park's of Hamilton	OU10GYO	Stagecoach	T900SGB	South Gloucestershire
LSK870	Park's of Hamilton	PO12GWG	Travellers Choice	WA10ENK	Chalfont (Northampton)
MIG9437	National Express	PO12GWJ	Travellers Choice	WA10ENL	Chalfont (Northampton)

WA10ENM	Chalfont (Northampton)	YN10FKR	Selwyns / Haytons	YT12YUS	Excalibur
WA57JZT	Chalfont (Northampton)	YN10FKS	Selwyns / Haytons	YX08FYP	East Yorkshire
WA59EBC	Chalfont (Northampton)	YN10FKT	Selwyns / Haytons	YY63OEJ	East Yorkshire
WA60DZG	Chalfont (Northampton)	YN10FKV	Selwyns / Haytons	YY63OEK	East Yorkshire
WA61AKF	Chalfont (Northampton)	YN11AYA	Selwyns / Haytons	YY63OEL	East Yorkshire
WA61AKP	Chalfont (Northampton)	YN11AYB	Selwyns / Haytons	YY63OEM	East Yorkshire
WA61AKU	Chalfont (Northampton)	YN11AYC	Selwyns / Haytons	YY63OEN	East Yorkshire
WF63LTA	Chalfont (Northampton)	YN11AYD	Selwyns / Haytons	YY63OEO	East Yorkshire
WF63LTE	Chalfont (Northampton)	YN60ABX	Stagecoach	YY63OJA	East Yorkshire
WX07OVJ	Skills	YN60ACF	Stagecoach	YY63OJB	East Yorkshire
YN10FKM	Selwyns / Haytons	YN60ACJ	Stagecoach	YY63OJC	East Yorkshire
YN10FKO	Selwyns / Haytons	YN60ACO	Stagecoach	YY63OJD	East Yorkshire
YN10FKP	Selwyns / Haytons	YN60ACU	Stagecoach		

ISBN 9781904875 80 2   © Published by British Bus Publishing Ltd, November 2015

British Bus Publishing Ltd, 16 St Margaret's Drive, Telford, TF1 3PH

Telephone: 01952 255669

web; www.britishbuspublishing.co.uk
e-mail: sales@britishbuspublishing.co.uk